ENDURING
L I E S

*The Rwandan Genocide
in the Propaganda System,
20 Years Later*

The Real News Books

Edward S. Herman and David Peterson

The Real News Books

ISBN-13: 978-1500751111
ISBN-10: 1500751111

Layout/Design: Alphabet Soup
Evergreen Park, IL 60805

Printed in the United States of America

CONTENTS

CONTENTS

Maps:

Preface

According to the widely accepted history of the 1994 "Rwandan genocide," there existed a plan or conspiracy among members of Rwanda's Hutu majority to exterminate the country's minority Tutsi population. This plan, the story goes, was hatched some time prior to the April 6, 1994 assassination of Rwandan President Juvénal Habyarimana, who died when his Falcon 50 jet was shot-down as it approached the airport of the capital city of Kigali. The killers allegedly responsible for this crime were "Hutu Power" extremists in positions of authority at the time. Although Habyarimana was Hutu, the story continues, he was also more moderate and accommodative toward the Tutsi than "Hutu Power" extremists could tolerate; they were therefore forced to physically eliminate him in order to carry out their plan to exterminate the Tutsi. The mass killings of Tutsi and "moderate Hutu" swiftly followed over the next 100 days, with perhaps 800,000 or as many as 1.1 million deaths. The "Rwandan genocide" came to an end only when the armed forces of Paul Kagame's Rwandan Patriotic Front drove the *"génocidaires"* from power, and liberated the country.

We refer to the above-version of the events that transpired in Rwanda 1994 as the *standard model* of the "Rwandan genocide." And we note, up front, that we believe that this model is a complex of interwoven lies which, when examined closely, unravels *in toto*.

Nevertheless, its Truth has been entered into the establishment history books and promulgated within the field of genocide studies, in documentaries, in the official history at the International Criminal Tribunal for Rwanda, and even proclaimed from on-high by the UN Security Council in April 2014.

The institutionalization of the "Rwandan genocide" has been the remarkable achievement of a propaganda system sustained by both public and private power, with the crucial assistance of a related cadre of intellectual enforcers. The favorite weapons of these enforcers are reciting the institutionalized untruths as gospel while portraying critics of the standard model as "genocide deniers," dark figures who lurk at the same moral level as child molesters, to be condemned and even outlawed. But we will show that this is not only crude name-calling, it also deflects attention away from those figures who bear the greatest responsibility for the bulk of the killings in Rwanda 1994, and for the even larger-scale killings in Zaire and the Democratic Republic of Congo thereafter.

Our book draws upon the work of a number of critics of the standard model, as well as the steadily growing stock of revelations that have entered the public realm over the past 20 years. But we also cite the publications of many of this model's defenders who, though failing to question and free themselves from the early deluge of propaganda about the "genocide," have still produced important studies on Rwanda or central Africa more broadly, and we cite them in their areas of strength. (The Belgian scholar Filip Reyntjens stands-out in this respect.) In other cases, however, we deal with writers who advocate so zealously on behalf of the standard model that they and their work are notable for entirely different reasons—as willful conveyers of misinformation on Rwanda 1994, and, ultimately, as propagandists for Kagame Power. (The Canadian writer Gerald Caplan and the British writer Linda Melvern are featured here, but they are far from alone.)

In the research, acquisition of documents, and writing of the present book, our greatest debts are to the Canadian attorney Christopher Black and the U.S. attorney Peter Erlinder, both of whom have represented Hutu defendants before the International Criminal Tribunal for Rwanda in two of its major trials, the Military II and Military I trials, respectively. We've also been guided by the work of the Canadian analyst of Rwanda, Robin Philpot. Leopold Nsengiyumva (Rwanda) and Lauren Tipton (United States), both of whom served as legal assistants on Christopher Black's team before the ICTR, among others, also provided us with assistance. As has the U.S. reference librarian Dale Wertz (indeed, over many years).

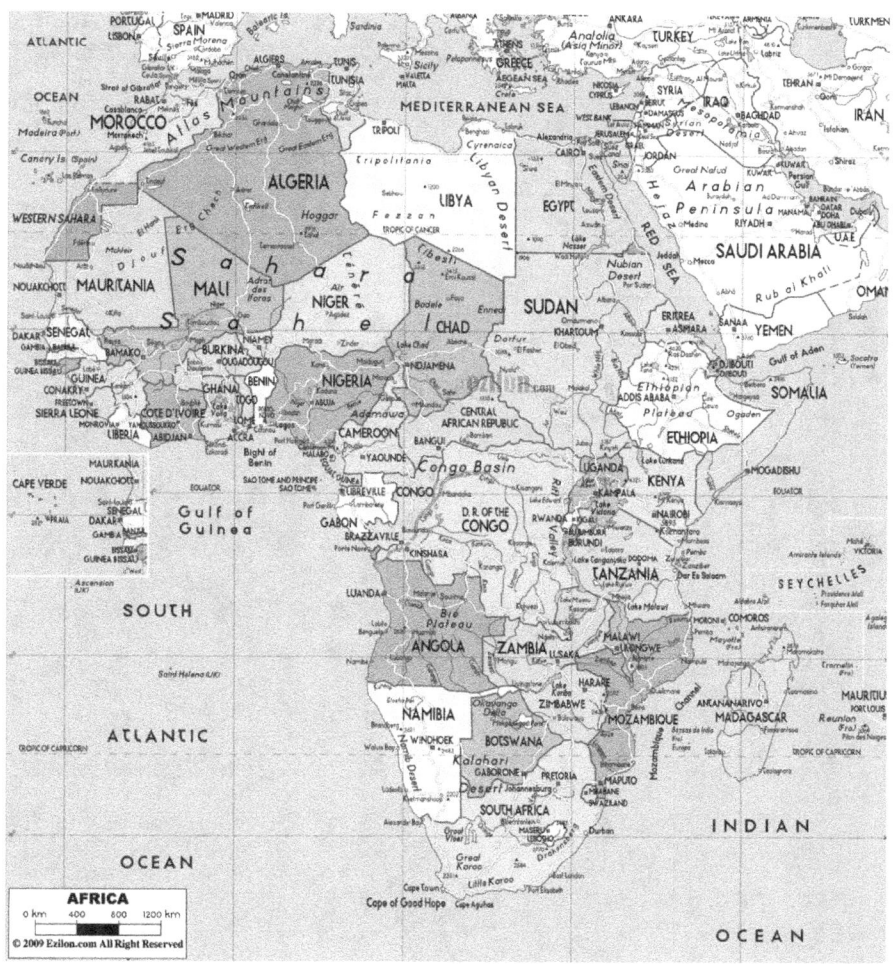

Map of Africa, derived from EZILON MAPS

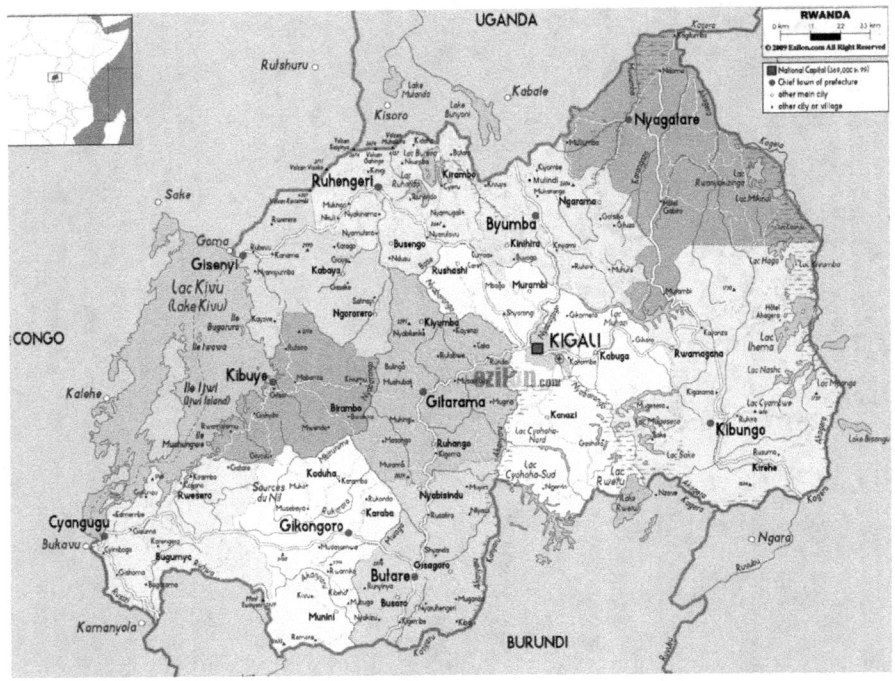

Map of Rwanda 1994, derived from EZILON MAPS

Introduction

This year in April marked the twentieth anniversary of the 1994 mass killings in Rwanda. Once again, the "Rwandan genocide" became a hot topic.[1] Its anniversary was officially commemorated in Kigali by the government of Paul Kagame and by governments around the world; by the United Nations, which since 2004 had named April 7 the Day of Remembrance of the Victims of the Rwanda Genocide; by genocide and holocaust scholars and by the United States Holocaust Memorial Museum in Washington; and by an International Forum on Genocide held in Kigali. It was also commemorated by countless local groups on and off university campuses formed on an *ad hoc* basis; by the establishment media globally; and by left- and liberal-interventionist intellectuals and political figures, always eager to cite the "necessity to intervene" and lament the "consequences of non-intervention."[2]

As a way of kicking-off the year, the *New York Times* on January 10 published a column by Michael Dobbs titled "Rwanda's Shrouded Nightmare."[3] "It is now commonly recognized that the international community failed miserably in its efforts to protect the people of Rwanda," Dobbs observed. "Whether the genocide was planned, and was thus foreseeable, has been hotly debated by scholars, politicians and lawyers."

In conjunction with his column, this emissary from the Holocaust Memorial Museum, where Dobbs runs the Rwanda Documentation and Oral History project, posted something called "The Rwanda 'Genocide Fax'" to the websites of both the Museum[4] and the National Security Archive[5] at George Washington University, the first installment in what was intended to be a joint, year-long project between the Archive and the Museum's Center for the Prevention of Genocide. Drawing on a collection of 26 documents, and accompanied by a lengthy analysis by Dobbs, Dobbs wrote that a fax (an encrypted or coded cable) was sent by Canadian Lieut.-General and force commander of the United Nations Assistance Mission in Rwanda (UNAMIR) Roméo Dallaire on January 11, 1994, from Kigali to the Department of Peacekeeping Operations at the United Nations in New York City. This fax allegedly warned the UN of an "anti-Tutsi extermination" plot that had been hatched by extremist Hutu figures. (We discuss the authenticity of this fax in Section 10, below.)

The Museum also sponsored a series of events on "Rwanda 20 Years Later."[6] Among these was a program with Philip Gourevitch, one of the earliest disseminators of the "Genocide Fax" in the English-language media,[7] as well as the United Nation's Office on Genocide Prevention and the Responsibility to Protect, devoted to what the Museum described as the "leaders who instigated violence, the individuals who participated willingly in mass murder, and the international community that looked away."[8] Some weeks later, on April 30, at the Museum's National Tribute Dinner and "in conjunction with Holocaust Days of Remembrance events in Washington," Dallaire himself received the 2014 Elie Wiesel Award for his "valiant attempts to warn the world of and prevent the 1994 genocide in Rwanda, despite enormous apathy and opposition from the UN, the United States, and the rest of the international community."[9]

Since 1994, the alleged "failure" on the part of the United States and its allies to react decisively to the "Rwandan genocide" (likewise with the "Bosnian genocide"[10]), even though these powers had allegedly been warned about the grave threats facing the country's Tutsi minority, and allegedly learned within the first few days of the event that the Hutu had launched their planned genocide against the Tutsi, has served an important role in justifying U.S. and Western allies' power-projection in Africa and elsewhere.

This is one of the most frequently recurring and widely accepted truths in the standard model of what happened in Rwanda in 1994 (and in earlier and later years as well). Within the Western propaganda system, these truths have long been institutionalized and insulated from challenge—and anybody who tries to challenge them, no matter how seriously, and with how much evidence to the contrary, is dismissed as a "genocide denier." But, to a remarkable degree, the truths embodied in this model are untrue and often the inverse of the truth, attributing villainy to the victims of the events of 1994, and making the real villains into heroes and saviors and, now, elder statesmen.

The extent to which the Western propaganda system bends in favor of anyone whose actions serve Western—especially U.S.—geopolitical interests is captured in this set of facts: That Paul Kagame twice has won elections in Rwanda, with 95 percent of the reported vote in 2003, and 93 percent in 2010, although the Tutsi population of Rwanda which he allegedly saved from Hutu killers is only some 10 percent of the total, and the Hutu population which he at the same time conquered comprise close to 90 percent (with Twa making up the rest). Disappearances, assassinations, and extended prison sentences for opposition political figures and journalists, and the banning of opposition political parties, have been regular features of a 20-year-long Kagame-Rwandan Patriotic Front (RPF[11]) "regime consolidation" and the ascendency of Kagame Power.[12] Were U.S. targets such as Russia's President Vladimir Putin or Venezuela's late President Hugo Chavez or any number of successive Iranian presidents ever to have been awarded 93 or 95 percent of the reported votes in an election, the establishment U.S. media would have devoted huge, angry, and sarcastic denunciations to such a display of electoral corruption, and rejected and delegitimized the outcomes. But Kagame's flagrantly corrupt victories and the brutal means his RPF has employed to guarantee them have hardly caused a dent in his recognition as a respectable and legitimate leader. He has been described as the "Abraham Lincoln" of a new and emancipated Africa,[13] and a "model for the rest of Africa and the World."[14] Western celebrities flock to visit with him and like to appear with him in public. And he is regularly feted at public events as a cosmopolitan man of great wisdom and a defender of human rights, as when in late September 2013, he appeared on stage with Elie Wiesel at Cooper Union in New York City,[15] or when in late April 2014, he appeared at the Milken Institute Global Conference in Los Angeles, and shared the stage with Tony Blair.[16]

Let us first briefly review some relevant events in Rwandan history prior to the 1990s, and then turn a critical eye towards the major lies that have underpinned and sustained the twentieth anniversary memorial circus of the "Rwandan genocide."

1. Rwanda: Background and context

"The 1990s began with a great surge of hope," the *Human Development Report* for 1991 opened. "Democracy swept across Eastern Europe and the Soviet Union. The Berlin Wall came down. Germany was reunited. One-party systems were on the retreat in Africa. A new era of human rights seemed to be dawning."[17]

Leaving aside this report's blindly optimistic and even millenarian tone, for the tiny (slightly smaller than Massachusetts) central African country of Rwanda, the 1990s began on October 1, 1990, when an armed group of between 2,000 and 4,000 Tutsi members of the Ugandan People's Defense Force, calling themselves the Rwandan Patriotic Front, invaded northern Rwanda, launching what would become a 46 month war against the government in Kigali, and culminating in the massive bloodshed and losses of lives of the April - July, 1994 period.

The RPF was founded in Kampala, Uganda, in late 1987, when the leaders of an earlier organization of Tutsi exiles from Rwanda, called the Rwanda Alliance for National Unity, decided to rename and reorient the organization's public profile in an attempt to appeal to a larger base of supporters. Gone was the earlier Marxist revolutionary edge. Instead, they issued a practical Eight Point Plan, and reiterated the right of return of all Tutsi refugees whose families had been fleeing Rwanda since the 1960s, after the Hutu revolution of 1959-1961 overthrew the last Tutsi king,[18] abolished the monarchy, and, most important, established majority Hutu rule.

Rwanda had been a kingdom since the 14th century, and remained one even during the period of first German (1890-1916) and then Belgian (1916-1962) colonial rule. The territory in central Africa east of Lake Kivu that would become the Kingdom of Rwanda was settled sometime prior to the 1300s by groups of Bantu language-speakers later known as Kinyarwanda. Of these Kinyarwanda speakers, two groups emerged: A small group of aboriginal pigmies known as Twa, and a large group of Banyarwandans. Throughout the nearly 600 year history of the Kingdom, a class structure developed such that if a Banyarwandan person was privileged within the society, this person came to be identified as "Tutsi;" conversely, if a Banyarwandan person was non-privileged and socially subordinated to the "Tutsi," this person came to be identified as a "Hutu." The "ethnic" patina on this fundamental division of social identities became increasingly polarized from the second-half of the 19th Century on;[19] with the layers of many generations now built-up upon it, it survives till this day, more rigid than ever. And because the Kingdom was highly stratified—indeed, this feature of the Kingdom was exacerbated and exploited under both German and Belgian colonial rule—it was the Belgian authorities, after all, that in the 1930s created the notorious practice of issuing "ethnic" identity cards—there were fewer persons at the top who enjoyed political and economic power, and many more non-privileged persons below them who did not. Mahmood Mamdani sums-up the meaning of "Tutsi" and "Hutu" quite nicely: "To be a Tutsi was thus to be in power, near power, or simply to be identified with power—just as to be a Hutu was more and more to be a subject."[20] Hence, the conflicts and struggles between the "Tutsi" minority and the "Hutu" majority that remain absolutely central to Rwandan history, as well as to the histories of neighboring Burundi, Uganda, the Democratic Republic of Congo, and Tanzania.

After the Second World War, the Kingdom of Rwanda was not only a Belgian colony, it also became a Trust Territory of the United Nations. (Just as the Kingdom had been a mandate of the League of Nations up till this time.) In the postwar period, this meant one thing above all else: Sooner or later, independence from colonial rule would come to the Kingdom. But in the 1950s, this meant something else as well: Social organizing on the part of the Hutu majority, the creation of the first political parties in the country's history, and pressures for democratization and open political competition. In 1957, nine Hutu intellectuals published the *Hutu Manifesto*. "The problem is above all a problem of political monopoly which is held by one race, the Tutsi," the *Manifesto* stated, strangely treating a longstanding class conflict within the Kingdom's social order ("Tutsi" v. "Hutu") not only as an "ethnic" conflict, but as a "racial" one. "[G]iven the totality of current structures, [this political monopoly] becomes an economic and social monopoly....[And] given the *de facto* discrimination in education, [it] ends up being a cultural monopoly. To the great despair of the Hutu who see themselves condemned to remain forever manual laborers or worse....."[21]

By late 1959, a major Hutu liberation movement was underway, fueled by the proliferation of the new, alternative Hutu-run media and new Hutu political parties that had formed, most notably Grégoire Kayibanda's Party of the Movement and of Hutu Emancipation (PARMEHUTU). "Rwanda was a simmering cauldron," Catharine Newbury writes.[22] In Rwanda then as much as today, with 83 percent of the population identi-

15

fying themselves as "Hutu," and 16.5 percent as "Tutsi," democratization in turn meant that the "explosive potential of ethnic voting blocks in direct popular elections could not be ignored."[23] When acts of Tutsi-on-Hutu and Hutu-on-Tutsi political violence began in late 1959, the Belgian authorities responded in a way that they had never done before: Now, the Belgians sided with the Hutu. Gérard Prunier quotes the Belgian Colonel Guy Logiest, who had been sent to Rwanda to oversee the eventual transition of power: "Some among my assistants thought I was wrong in being so partial against the Tutsi," Logiest wrote in his memoir. "Today, twenty-five years later, I ask myself what was it that made me act with such resolution. It was without doubt the will to give the people back their dignity."[24]

By "people," Logiest meant "Hutu people." Acts of interethnic violence escalated rapidly, in particular, Hutu attacks on Tutsi settlements. Decades- and sometimes centuries-old Tutsi privileges were suddenly being overturned and taken away. The Tutsi exodus from Rwanda began in 1960. Communal elections were held in June and July. Out of 229 communes, Hutu candidates won 211 of them.[25] Then in January 1961, at a large meeting of Hutu burgomasters in Gitarama city, at which both Logiest and Kayibanda were also present, the Kingdom of Rwanda was dissolved (the so-called *"Coup d'État de Gitarama"*), and the Republic of Rwanda proclaimed in its place. In September, amid ongoing political violence, elections were held for the national legislature. The PARME-HUTU received 78 percent of the vote, while a Tutsi party, the Rwandese National Union, received 17 percent, the outcome more or less reflecting the ethnic composition of Rwanda at the time. (Recall that in our day, Tutsi leader Paul Kagame twice has won presidential elections with more than 90 percent of the reported vote.) The national legislature belonged to the Hutu majority. There followed Grégoire Kayibanda's election to the presidency in October—another major Hutu victory. (Kayibanda would be overthrown by the Hutu General Juvénal Habyarimana in the so-called bloodless coup of July 5, 1973; later, he and his wife were literally starved to death by the Habyarimana regime.[26]) Rwanda's independence from Belgian rule was finally declared on July 1, 1962.[27] A Hutu-dominated Rwanda had been born, with Belgium acting as the midwife to this newly independent country.

The Tutsi exodus from Rwanda continued throughout the 1960s, largely to Burundi, but also in lesser numbers to Uganda, Zaire, and Tanzania, and to Belgium, France, Canada, and the United States. So did armed Tutsi guerrilla attacks on Rwanda from southern Uganda by fighters who called themselves *Inyenzi* ("cockroaches") because they were active at night but disappeared with the daylight. Such attacks provoked additional backlashes against the Tutsi who still remained in Rwanda, causing more to flee the country. By 1967, around 70,000 Tutsi exiles had settled in Uganda, and some 118,000 by 1985.[28] Among these exile-refugees were the families of many of the Tutsi who, from October 1, 1990 on, took-up arms in Uganda and invaded Rwanda, precipitating the devastating war of 1990-1994.

One year after the Ugandan dictator Idi Amin was overthrown in 1979, Milton Obote, whose first presidency had been overthrown by Amin in 1971, won a new election and assumed the presidency for a second time. Within weeks of Obote's December 1980 victory, Uganda's former defense minister, Yoweri Museveni, along with 26 others, launched a guerrilla war against the Obote regime. Eventually calling themselves the National Resistance Army (NRA), two of Museveni's closest comrades in this campaign had been very young boys when their families fled Rwanda in the early 1960s, and had first fought under Museveni in 1978-1979, as part of the effort to drive Amin from power: Fred Rwigyema and Paul Kagame. "Persecution drove many young Banyarwanda into the NRA, the insurgent force led by Museveni," Catharine Watson has written. "By 1984, Banyarwanda were probably the third largest group in the NRA....More joined, many of them refugees, when the NRA occupied western Uganda in November 1984....When the NRA captured Kampala on January 26, 1986, it had 14,000 men, an estimated 2,000 – 3,000 of whom were Banyarwanda."[29]

Rwigyema, a highly respected military leader who at one point had risen to the rank of army chief of staff under Museveni, before an anti-Tutsi backlash in Uganda impelled Museveni to demote him in 1989, led the RPF's October 1990 invasion of Rwanda, where he died of a gunshot wound to the head on only the second day.

But Kagame's fortunes have followed the opposite trajectory. Like Rwigyema, Kagame flourished under Museveni, eventually becoming

Uganda's director of military intelligence until he, too, was demoted in 1989. When the RPF invaded Rwanda, Kagame was taking a one-year military science course at the United States Army Command and Staff College at Fort Leavenworth, Kansas; and when he learned of Rwigyema's death several days after the event, he withdrew from the course and made his way back to the RPF in the field, where he assumed command of a badly beaten guerrilla campaign on the verge of collapsing.[30]

What is more, the Tutsi members of the NRA who later became members of the RPF even while, remarkably, they had remained within the Ugandan People's Defense Force, and retained Museveni's full support,[31] always understood that their years of service under Museveni were training and preparation for their real mission: The recapture of Rwanda from its Hutu majority, to whom their Tutsi elders had lost control of the country during the 1959-1961 revolution. As the onetime RPF Secretary-General and Kagame loyalist Tito Rutaremara explained: "All during the 1960s and 70s, there was this vague idea to go back, but no strategy, no leaders....We decided [from 1987 on] we'd have to fight the dictatorship. Fighting to go back was the only way. If you negotiated with the dictatorship and then go back, they would put you in prison or worse. No, we have to remove the dictatorship in Rwanda. Only through that can we have peace."[32]

By "we," Rutaremara meant "Tutsi." From then on, this has been both the Rwandan Patriotic Front's and Paul Kagame's conscious reason-for-being. And though in their official statements, the RPF was always careful to prioritize the right of return of the Tutsi refugees, and not to mention the overthrowing of the Hutu majority regime, which they believe stole the country from its rightful owners back in 1959-1961, when the Habyarimana government in Kigali began to take steps to address the Tutsi refugee problem from 1988 on,[33] for the RPF, this was the final straw: The RPF had to attack *now* and *pre-emptively* to recapture the country, before Habyarimana could remove from the RPF's propaganda arsenal the right-of-return objection to his regime.

A critical feature of the years 1990 through the large-scale killing in Rwanda in 1994 was the U.S. and allied support of Kagame. This extended from training him and implicitly sanctioning the RPF's 1990 invasion and subsequent guerilla war in Rwanda, to protecting him from any UN sanctions and later, in 1994, sponsoring a Tribunal that would serve his plans for anti-Hutu vengeance and pro-RPF dictatorship propaganda. In addition, the United States and its allies worked hard in the early 1990s to weaken the Habyarimana government, forcing the abandonment of many of the economic and social gains from the 1959 revolution, undermining Habyarimana's popularity and helping to reinforce the Tutsi minority's economic power. Eventually, the RPF was able to achieve a legal military presence inside Rwanda thanks to a series of ceasefires and other agreements that led to the final Peace Agreement signed by the Rwandan government and the RPF in Arusha, Tanzania, on August 4, 1993.[34]

Pressed upon the Rwandan government by the United States and Britain, the Arusha Accords called for the creation of a power-sharing, Broad-Based Transitional Government until national elections could be held in 1995 (i.e., within 22 months of the signing of the final Peace Agreement), the repatriation and resettlement of refugees and internally displaced persons, the "integration" of the armed forces of Rwanda and the RPF, and the introduction of a Neutral International Force to provide security during the transition period, among other terms. Under the "Integration of the Armed Forces" agreement reached on the final day of negotiations, the new Rwandan military's chain of command was to be divided evenly (fifty-fifty) between government forces and the RPF, with alternation between the two at specific dates; for lower ranking forces, the government would supply 60 percent of the personnel, and the RPF 40 percent.[35] As the Canadian Rwanda analyst Robin Philpot notes, with terms such as these, the Accords gave the invading RPF "much more power than the people would ever give it in free elections," with the result that that country's entire civil service disintegrated between September 1993 and April 1994.[36] In short, the Arusha Accords positioned the RPF for its imminent and bloody overthrow of a relatively democratic coalition government and the takeover of the Rwandan state by an unelected Tutsi minority dictatorship.

It is also of relevance to developments in Rwanda that on October 21, 1993, in Burundi, Rwanda's southern neighbor and a country with roughly the same ethnic composition as Rwanda (90 percent Hutu, 10 percent Tutsi), Burundi's almost exclusively Tutsi military leadership assassinated President Melchior Ndadaye, and retook control of the state. Burundi's first-ever Hutu president, Ndadaye had been democratically elected less than five months before, on June 1, with some 65 percent of the reported vote. In the parliamentary elections that followed on June 29, his party, *Front pour la Démocratie au Burundi* (FRODEBU), had gone on to receive 71.4 percent of the votes, and captured 65 out of 81 total seats.[37] In Burundi, free elections in 1993 had enabled the country's Hutu majority to assert itself and win majority representation.

The news of Ndadaye's death triggered a massive bloodbath over the next several weeks in which perhaps as many as 50,000 people perished, with both Hutu on Tutsi massacres and the Tutsi military's massacres of Hutu. Perhaps as many as 580,000 Burundians fled the country during the first few weeks, with another 1,000,000 people internally displaced by the conflict; by March 1994, 260,000 of these mostly Hutu refugees remained in Rwanda.[38] At the time of this coup, in late 1993, there already were some 350,000 people still internally displaced in Rwanda as a result of the RPF's major military offensive of January and February that year;[39] the new inflow of refugees from Burundi further destabilized conditions there. In the words of a cable sent out widely from the U.S. Embassy in Kigali, everyone had gained a greater "understanding of the intimate link between what happens in Burundi and the security situation in Rwanda."[40]

The full impact of the Burundian coup was felt not only materially, but psychologically as well. And not just inside Burundi. René Lemarchand, a French-American expert on Africa's Great Lakes region, traces the links between Burundi and Rwanda even further back, to the massacre (though Lemarchand prefers the term 'genocide') of perhaps 200,000 Hutu in Burundi by the country's ruling Tutsi party in 1972. Lemarchand quotes a Rwandan Hutu clergyman, who in late 1993, told him: "When we told [Rwanda's Hutu youth] not to spill blood [in the aftermath of the assassination of Ndadaye on October 21], they said, 'Look, since 1972 it is our blood that's being spilled! Now we hear that President Ndadaye has been killed. If they did that, that means that we are next!'"[41]

By "they," Rwanda's Hutu youth meant the "Tutsi" minority of both Burundi—and, of course, the RPF. In his memoir of the year that he spent as the force commander of UNAMIR, Roméo Dallaire notes the "contrast" that he himself experienced "between the almost sunny optimism of Kigali in August and the somber capital I returned to on October 22,"[42] the day after the coup. Although the coup was reversed and several of its principals fled to Kampala, where they stayed "as well-received guests of RPF circles between late October 1993 and early February 1994,"[43] a confidential State Department assessment of the situation warned that the "violence could spread....The failed coup heightens ethnic enmity in Rwanda....Rwandan Hutu, who fear a Tutsi takeover, and Tutsi, who fear being victims of a bloodbath by the majority, are riveted on events in Burundi." The assessment added that "The failed coup....makes implementation of the peace settlement in neighboring Rwanda more questionable...."[44]

In fact, for reasons we discuss in the sections that follow, implementation of the Arusha Accords largely never occurred, but one exception does stand out. In Article 72 of the Protocol on the Integration of the Armed Forces of the Two Parties, we read that "In order to participate in catering for the security of its personalities, the RPF shall bring to Kigali a security unit whose size is equivalent of one (1) Infantry Battalion of six hundred people."[45] With these terms in mind, Dallaire's description of operation "Clean Corridor," UNAMIR's securing a "safe spot" for the RPF's military and political personnel to live when they arrived in Kigali in late December 1993, is very revealing. Out of the four possible locations that Dallaire recommended, the "worst" option was chosen: The National Council for Development (CND). The CND is a complex of buildings in Kigali that includes the Rwandan National Assembly building, a hotel complex (where the RPF would set up its base), and a convention center. "Imagine," Dallaire writes, "a rebel organization being given control of the East and West blocks on Parliament Hill, or a portion of the Capitol complex in Washington. The appearance was all wrong." Later, Dallaire continues: "Once the RPF began digging in, they never stopped for the next four months....By the time the war resumed in April, they had built an underground complex under the CND. It was clear that while the peace process was progressing, they were also prepared for the alternative."[46]

As usual, Dallaire either misses or deliberately suppresses the real lesson of the information he conveys. The RPF was never interested in the "peace process"—it was, however, wholly committed to the "alternative." And it would permit nothing to stand in the way of completing its mission.

2. The RPF invasion and low-level aggressive war that never was a "civil war"

When Roméo Dallaire was sent to Rwanda in August 1993 on a reconnaissance mission to learn what a UN peacekeeping force would need to help implement the Arusha Accords, his team assessed the capabilities of both the FAR [*Forces Armées Rwandaises*, Rwanda's national army] and the RPF. Dallaire's report back to the UN was striking. "The RPF victory, in its last offensive [February 1993], has adversely affected the morale of the [FAR]," he wrote. "The general standard of [FAR] training…is low… Soldiers possess only basic military skills of varying standards… A large number of weapons were stolen or lost during the war… The organization must be rebuilt."[47]

But whereas Dallaire concluded that FAR's overall capability was "medium to low," not so the RPF's. The RPF had "approximately 20,000 armed soldiers," he wrote. (By April 1994, their numbers would be greater.) The RPF had a "very high morale and discipline. They are a young army (average age estimated at 16 years with most field commanders under 30). Their leadership is respected by their men….[A] very effective training system." The RPF is a "well led, effective, disciplined force," Dallaire summed-up his assessment. Most strikingly, he concluded that "They displayed the potential to easily defeat the [FAR]."[48]

The rapid victory of Kagame's RPF after the assassination of Habyarimana marked the final offensive in their 46-month-war to take over Rwanda.[49] But the RPF's aggression was never condemned by the United States or addressed as such by the Security Council. Moreover, it was followed by a series of U.S. and British moves that helped the aggressor penetrate the Rwandan government and military (the essence of the Arusha Accords), infiltrate armed cells into Kigali and elsewhere,[50] and eventually place an oversized and well-equipped security battalion on the grounds of the National Council for Development complex in Kigali, with between 4,000 and 6,000 armed fighters in Kigali alone—all in preparation for ongoing guerrilla strikes and, of course, the final assault.

In fact, following the April 6, 1994 shooting down of Habyiramana's jet, the RPF was able to expand the territory it controlled at a prodigious pace, doubling its size within 24 hours.[51] Within two weeks, the RPF controlled the northeastern-third of Rwanda. "[T]he [FAR] troops were running for their lives," is how Dallaire describes the FAR's response to the RPF's offensive.[52] By May 25, the RPF controlled one-half of Rwanda, and had Kigali encircled from without and subverted from within. By early July, the RPF controlled two-thirds of Rwanda, including Kigali. And by July 18—the date on which the RPF declared victory—it controlled all of Rwanda (with the exception of the far southwest, which the French forces of Operation Turquoise had occupied and would control until their departure in late August).

Meanwhile, back in Kigali, the Rwandan government and its various forces were in complete disarray at the time of Habyarimana's death. In a state of crisis and chaos, an interim government was formed on April 9, after the killings had already begun; the interim government would flee Kigali within a week for the city of Gitarama, never to return. On the military side, Dallaire's summary of his intelligence officer Amadou Deme's mid-April assessment of the FAR's own chaotic state is revealing. FAR "troops were receiving very little tactical information or direction at the front; soldiers were deserting....Some troops wanted peace....[A] rift was starting between some military units and the Interahamwe. As anticipated, the [FAR] front-line troops and recruits, undisciplined and disorganized, would not put up much of a fight."[53] Throughout the months of April, May, and June, the interim government's representative at the United Nations pled for UNAMIR to be strengthened, and the FAR made one ceasefire offer after another to the RPF. But clearly winning the military struggle, the RPF consistently rejected both options.

That is to say, this armed conflict was never a "civil war," never an indigenous Tutsi rebellion against the repression and discrimination of Rwanda's ethnic minority by its post-1959-1961 Revolution's Hutu majority. On the contrary, it was a *foreign invasion* of Rwanda, led by young Rwandan and Ugandan Tutsi members of the Ugandan People's Defense Force (formerly the Ugandan National Resistance Army), which by 1987, had reconfigured themselves as the Rwandan Patriotic Front.

It is, therefore, quite revealing to find how the two *ad hoc* tribunals created by the Security Council in 1993 and 1994—the International Criminal Tribunal for the Former Yugoslavia(ICTY)[54] and the International Criminal Tribunal for Rwanda (ICTR)[55]—interpret the nature of the armed conflicts with which they have dealt. In the first indictment ever issued by the ICTR, drafted by Richard Goldstone against eight Hutu in 1995, Goldstone stated matter-of-factly: "At all times relevant to this indictment, there was an *internal* armed conflict occurring within Rwanda."[56] The same line has been repeated in one form or another ever since. For example, in the October 1997 indictment of Jean Kambanda, the acting prime minister of Rwanda's interim government from April 9, 1994 until he fled the country in July: "During the said events, there was a *non-international* armed conflict in the territory of Rwanda."[57] And in the December 1999 amended indictment of Col. Théoneste Bagosora: "During the events referred to in this indictment, a state of *non-international* conflict existed in Rwanda."[58] In short, although the 46 month armed conflict within Rwanda resulted from the Ugandan People's Defense Force-Rwandan Patriotic Front (UPDF-RPF) cross-border invasion and occupation of the country, official history via the ICTR and the advocates for the standard model systematically define the conflict as a *civil war*, rather than as an *international war*, and most certainly not as an act of *naked aggression* (in contrast, recall U.S. President George H.W. Bush's condemnation of Iraq's "naked aggression" against Kuwait only two months earlier[59]). —Why not?

We believe that the ICTR here is showing the kind of political imperatives under which it operates. Since the invasion of another country is a violation of the UN Charter as well as illegal under customary international law, for the ICTR to define the Rwandan conflict as an international one would have placed one party to the conflict, the UPDF-RPF, on the wrong side of international law, and not only during 1994, but from the October 1, 1990 date of the invasion. However, since the ICTR was established on the "victor's justice" model both to immunize the U.S. client-UPDF-RPF and to prosecute their Hutu victims exclusively, defining the conflict as an international one could never be permitted: Unlike Iraq's "naked aggression" against Kuwait, the UPDF-RPF's aggression against

Rwanda must remain non-international—a civil war or simply a military operation to stop the "genocide." The United States and Britain couldn't publicly support an illegal war, even if they supported it wholeheartedly and covertly; but they could support one side in a civil war that is alleged to be fighting to prevent the other side from committing genocide against its ethnic brethren. And as the revisionists-before-the-fact who made up the International Fact-Finding Commission (Alison Des Forges, William Schabas, *et al.*) had as early as March 1993 already begun to frame Rwanda's "head of state and...his immediate entourage, including members of his family" with accusations of "genocide,"[60] there was no doubting who were the good guys in this armed conflict, and who the bad.[61]

In the case of the Socialist Federal Republic of Yugoslavia (SFRY), on the other hand, there *was* a civil war in 1991, with the ethnic groups in the SFRY's six republics in conflict over whether to remain within the SFRY or to break-away from it. Then, by the historical engineering of the European Commission, a ruling was announced on November 20, 1991 to the effect that the "Socialist Federal Republic of Yugoslavia [was] in the process of dissolution,"[62] thus prejudging the outcome of this civil war in favor of the ethnic majorities in Slovenia, Croatia, Bosnia-Herzegovina, and Macedonia to withdraw these four republics from the SFRY. This was exactly what the Western powers wanted, and recognition of the newly independent states soon followed. But as the republics of Serbia and Montenegro as well as the vast majority of ethnic Serbs living in Croatia and Bosnia-Herzegovina opposed this outcome, Serbs became the bad guys. In this way, an ongoing civil war that had not been resolved (and would not be resolved until the Dayton Accords in late 1995) was legalistically transformed into an *international armed conflict*, framed as the "result of a plan conceived in Belgrade," with Serbs aggressing (or committing "naked aggression") against Croatia and Bosnia-Herzegovina.[63] Indeed, in the first trial ever conducted at the ICTY, that of a Bosnian Serb named Dusko Tadić, who was accused of murder and rape at a detention facility in Prijedor, Bosnia-Herzegovina, the prosecution devoted months to arguing the *international* nature of the Yugoslav wars.[64]

In both cases, U.S. and U.K. foreign policy objectives were advanced. (And in the case of the SFRY, European and NATO objectives were as well). When the Great Powers define a conflict as international (the

SFRY), it is not only an "international" conflict, but an "aggressive" war, and they can take actions about it, and try to use Chapter VII of the UN Charter and the Security Council to put the UN's stamp of approval on their actions. (At the time, and in contrast to the crises in Syria, Ukraine, and Iraq today, Boris Yeltsin's Russia was a nonfactor in the Security Council, and a rubber-stamp for the United States.) Conversely, when the Great Powers define a conflict as non-international (Rwanda), it is a "civil war," and they can shield this conflict from sanction under Chapter VII of the UN Charter, though they may interfere with and promote one side of it as they please. Thus does revisionism-before-the-fact serve the Great Powers. Kagame's RPF has been on a tear across the Great Lakes region of central Africa ever since.

3. "Hutu Power extremists" did not shoot-down Habyarimana's Falcon 50 jet

The assassination of Rwandan President Juvénal Habyarimana and Burundian President Cyprien Ntaryamira by the shooting-down of the former's Falcon 50 jet as it approached Kanombe International Airport on April 6, 1994 is widely regarded as the "triggering event" for the mass killings that followed. Michael Dobbs in his *New York Times* op-ed noted that the shoot-down was the "immediate trigger,"[65] but, strangely enough, he failed to say who pulled the trigger. In the standard model of the "Rwandan genocide"—the model accepted in Western capitals, by the Office of the Prosecutor at the ICTR, and in the field of Genocide Studies—the assassination was carried out by high-level "Hutu Power extremists," "desperate members" of Habyarimana's "own *akazu* circle," as Gérard Prunier put it back in 1995, "who had decided to gamble on their all-or-nothing 'final solution' scheme when they began to fear (or perhaps to know) that the President was finally going to comply with the provisions of the Arusha agreement."[66] (As if compliance with the terms of Arusha would not be far more threatening to RPF power!)

When it was created by UN Security Council Resolution 955 in late 1994, the ICTR was charged with (among other things) "prosecuting persons responsible for the genocide and other serious violations of international humanitarian law committed in the territory of Rwanda and…neighboring States, between 1 January 1994 and 31 December 1994…"[67]

Since the shooting-down of the presidential jet was a serious crime, and one with grave consequences far exceeding the event itself, it clearly falls within the ICTR's mandate. The late Australian lawyer Michael Hourigan, who led the "National Team" of roughly 20 investigators for the Office of the Prosecutor in 1996 and 1997, stated in a 2007 affidavit that the tribunal's original Chief Prosecutor Richard Goldstone had instructed his Team to "Identify the person(s) responsible for the fatal rocket attack on 6 April 1994 killing President Habyarimana and all others on board."[68] This was sometime in the spring of 1996.

The Canadian jurist Louise Arbour succeeded Goldstone as chief prosecutor at the ICTR (as well as at the Yugoslavia Tribunal) in October 1996. By early 1997, Hourigan's Team had been able to find three members of Kagame's RPF who volunteered information they deemed credible that it was Kagame who ordered the shoot-down of the jet. Hourigan communicated this to Arbour. "At no time did she suggest that our investigation was improper," his affidavit states. Ordered to fly to The Hague and meet with Arbour, Hourigan presented her with his evidence, a memo titled "Secret National Team Inquiry—Internal Memorandum." To his shock and surprise, Arbour became "aggressive" and skeptical toward his findings. She then instructed him that he was to terminate the investigation, and told him that the ICTR's "mandate only extended to events within the genocide, which in her view began 'after' the plane crash." "I was astounded at this statement," Hourigan's affidavit recounts. Thus was the "triggering event" ruled outside the ICTR's mandate, not by a decision of the court itself, but by the fiat of its chief prosecutor, who both here and in her work at the ICTY showed great responsiveness to U.S. policy interests. Hourigan's memo was confiscated—and has remained buried ever since. He returned to Kigali and resigned. Never again has the ICTR investigated the "triggering event."[69]

There is other evidence of Kagame-RPF responsibility for the shoot-down—and for U.S., British, Belgian, and Canadian roles in the event, and in the longstanding cover-up. French anti-terrorism Judge Jean-Louis Bruguière's detailed investigation on behalf of family members of the jet's crew came to the same conclusion as Hourigan, and led to his issuance of arrest warrants in November 2006 for nine members of the RPF, figures he accused of engaging in a "plot to physically eliminate the incumbent Rwandan President."[70] The "consistent line of testimony" was that the political situation was "not favorable to the hegemonic plans of Paul Kagame," so that his only solution was to assassinate Habyarimana and resume the war—exactly what did happen in Rwanda, April-July, 1994. As the Bruguière report puts it: "[D]ue to the numerical inferiority of the Tutsi electorate, the political balance of power did not allow [Kagame] to win elections on the basis of the political process set forth by the Arusha Agreements without the support of the opposition parties... .[I]n Paul Kagame's mind, the physical elimination of President Habyarimana became imperative as early as October 1993 as the sole way of achieving his political aims."[71]

Like Hourigan's, Bruguière's findings were built out of evidence provided by multiple defectors from the RPF, whose legions keep growing in number every year.[72] Many of these exiles from Kagame Power once held very high positions and were close to Kagame. With his penchant for political assassinations, particularly anyone with knowledge of his role in ordering the shoot-down of the Habyarimana jet, they live in constant fear for their lives.

One of them, the late Lieut. Abdul Ruzibiza, testified before Bruguière that "in February 1994 he formed part of the unit which was infiltrated in Kigali and which had the mission of carrying out reconnaissance of the Masaka-Kanombe sector,"[73] the area around the airport, in order to determine the best site from which to target the Habyarimana jet. Another, Sergeant Aloys Ruyenzi, testified that "as a member of the personal guard of Paul Kagame, he was in the meeting room at Mulindi headquarters on 31 March 1994, during a meeting between Paul Kagame and officers James Karabebe, Jacob Tumwine, Charles Karamba, Kayumba Nyamwasa and Théoneste Lizinde. According to his version of events, the meeting was held to plan the operational details of President Habyarimana's assassination."

This section of the Bruguière report continues:

[Ruyenzi] added that Paul Kagame stated "as soon as President Habyarimana leaves the Arusha meeting and his aircraft is approaching, fire on him. This war will not end until President Habyarimana is dead;"

Aloys Ruyenzi also claimed to have witnessed the delivery of two missiles to four soldiers who loaded them into a vehicle forming part of a convoy escorted by the UNAMIR which was destined for the C.N.D. in Kigali [i.e., site of the RPF headquarters in Kigali];

He added that Deputy-Lieutenant Frank Nziza and Corporal Eric Hakizamana were inside the vehicle and confided to him at the end of the war that they had participated in the attack. Eric Hakizamana fired the first missile which missed its target, Frank Nziza however succeeded in hitting and destroying the aircraft....[74]

According to former FBI counter-terrorism agent James Lyons, who was Commander of Investigations at the ICTR at the time of the Hourigan investigation, the National Team obtained information that both UN-AMIR as well as FAR soldiers had intercepted a radio message over an RPF channel on the evening of April 6 stating that "the target has been hit."[75]

Of the seven RPF figures named by Ruyenzi (excluding Kagame), Col. Théoneste Lizinde fled Rwanda as early as 1995 and was assassinated in Nairobi in 1996;[76] Kayumba Nyamwasa, once the army's chief of staff, fled to South Africa in 2010, and has survived multiple assassination attempts, one while he was recovering in a hospital from wounds suffered in the previous attempt.[77]

That Kagame organized the assassination of Habyarimana is entirely plausible strategically, as he could never have won the free election that was scheduled to be held within 22 months after the Arusha Accords and the formation of the Broad-Based Transitional Government, a move that Habyarimana was ready to implement. The immediacy with which RPF forces mobilized when news of the shoot-down reached their headquarters in Mulindi, and the complete disorder affecting the FAR at the same time, also contradict the standard model. As Theogene Rudasingwa, Kagame's one-time chief of staff, now living in exile, recalls a briefing he received from Kagame after the shoot-down: "[The] RPF was to explain to the international community how the Hutu extremists opposed to the Arusha peace Agreement were responsible for the shooting down of the plane, and had already started killing Tutsi and Hutu opposition politicians. According to this narrative, the government side had broken the ceasefire, and the RPF was resuming hostilities 1) to stop the killings and 2) to restore law and order."[78] In the words of another notorious liar: "If you tell a lie big enough and keep repeating it, people will eventually come to believe it."

It is amusing to watch the leading proponents of the standard model struggle on this issue, regularly pretending that the ICTR-Hourigan investigation and subsequent ICTR avoidance of this key issue never happened. Gerald Caplan, a veteran Canadian advocate for the Hutu "conspiracy to commit genocide" model as well as for Paul Kagame's and the RPF's positive image around the world, was the principal author of the Organization of African Unity's 2000 report *Rwanda: The Preventable Genocide*.[79] Although the OAU instructed the panel in charge of this inquiry to investigate "The killing of President Habyarimana of Rwanda on 6 April 1994,"[80] the panel punted: Never once in its report does the panel name who it believed was responsible for the assassination, although it mentions the event numerous times. "[W]ildly conflicting stories and accusations about the possible perpetrators have swirled ever since," the report states. "The truth is that to this day, this historic event is shrouded in conflicting rumors and accusations but no hard evidence. Mysteriously enough, a formal investigation of the crash has never been carried out, and this Panel has had no capacity to launch one."[81] In the end, the OAU inquiry recommended that the "OAU should ask the International Commission of Jurists to initiate an independent investigation" into the matter.[82]

Yet, when acting in his personal capacity as apologist for Kagame and the RPF, Caplan is less reticent: The findings of the RPF's own Committee of Experts' inquiry into the shoot-down "documents the logic most of us have accepted since the start. They pin the blame directly and fully on a group of Hutu extremists who were simply not prepared to accept the power-sharing provisions of the Arusha Accords."[83] Not surprisingly, the RPF's inquiry into the shoot-down exonerated the RPF and blamed "Hutu extremists."[84] So the conclusion is "logical" to Caplan.[85] As Filip

Reyntjens, a Belgian academic and onetime investigator for the ICTR, noted in his powerful demolition of the RPF's self-exoneration, Caplan is an "RPF supporter" whose assessment was a "painfully biased and uncritical endorsement."[86]

Linda Melvern, like Caplan, a long-standing advocate for the standard model who has also written about the shoot-down, never mentions the ICTR-Hourigan inquiry and its suppressed findings. Instead, she ponders over the "continuing secrecy of western nations, the withholding of evidence and the failure to conduct an international inquiry," all of which she calls "shocking."[87] That this could be a result of specific Western regimes—most notably the United States and Britain—protecting their own interests as well as that of their client Paul Kagame, never occurs to her. She searches for and finds people who say what she wants said— that the shoot-down was pure Hutu villainy. She even alleges an early call by Hutu *Radio Télévision Libre des Mille Collines* (RTLM) for action at the time of the assassination, but never mentions the readiness of the RPF and the extreme effectiveness of its forces, in contrast with FAR confusion and ineptitude.

"The international court established by the UN Security Council to try those responsible for genocide is silent on the assassination of Habyarimana," Melvern notes elsewhere, in an article titled "The Perfect Crime."[88] But as we've just seen, the ICTR did investigate this question, and having found the evidence disagreeable, its chief prosecutor, after having consulted the U.S. Embassy, closed it down. "The event is ruled outside the court's mandate on the grounds that the trial judges, in all their rulings, have confirmed the existence of a planned and systematically organised conspiracy to commit genocide," Melvern added, telling one Big Lie after another. "The court has determined that the mass killings could not be considered 'a spontaneous reaction' to the assassination of Habyarimana."

In contrast with Melvern's oft-repeated lie that all of the ICTR's judgments "have confirmed the existence of a planned and systematically organized conspiracy to commit genocide" (in fact, the opposite is the case, as we show in detail below), what makes the shoot-down a "perfect crime" is that it was carried out in service to the United States by one of its clients, Paul Kagame's RPF. Moreover, it is the Prosecution that refuses to touch the question of responsibility for the assassination, not because it lies outside the ICTR's mandate, but because the Prosecution knows what the answer would be, and it doesn't dare run the risk of permitting this.

4. The "Rwandan genocide" by the numbers

A universal refrain of the spokespersons for the standard model states that "Between April and July 1994, hundreds of thousands of persons, mostly Tutsi and moderate Hutus, were killed throughout Rwanda."[89]

Many conflicting estimates exist as to the number and ethnic composition of the Rwandans who perished during the months of April through July, 1994, during which the "genocide" took place. Also, many factors complicate reaching a definitive total, not the least of which is that RPF killings of Hutu continued unabated after the RPF seized power in July, and we have always suspected that these post-"genocide" deaths have been pulled backwards in time, and counted for the April-July period, rather than when they occurred.

The December 1999 UN Carlsson report for the Secretary-General stated that "Approximately 800,000 persons were killed during the 1994 genocide in Rwanda."[90] In 2004, the Rwandan Ministry of Local Government, Community Development and Social Affairs estimated 1,074,017 persons had died at the time.[91] In 2008, the Genocide Survivors Students Association of Rwanda estimated 1,952,087[92]—and even this total has been superseded by higher (i.e., even more outlandish) estimates.

A very serious ongoing research project named GenoDynamics, led by Christian Davenport and Allan Stam of the University of Michigan's Political Science Department, more conservatively estimates that "around 500,000" persons perished during the April – July 1994 period.[93] But more disturbing to the advocates for the standard model, these researchers also draw the important conclusion that a much greater number of Hutu died in Rwanda in 1994 than Tutsi. To this they add the important point, equally disturbing to advocates for the standard model, that the higher the total number of deaths in Rwanda, the greater the disparity between the relative (greater) number of Hutu and Tutsi deaths will also turn out to be. Finally, they have been arguing for at least the past ten years that that spikes in civilian casualties correlated with surges in RPF advances during the April – July, 1994 period.[94]

GenoDynamics estimates that the pre-April 1994 Tutsi component of the Rwandan population was approximately 500,000 persons. (There are higher estimates in circulation, of course, including one that we've used in the past—596,387—drawn from Rwanda's 1991 Census.[95]) GenoDynamics then takes an estimate of post-"genocide" Tutsi survivors of the April – July period from IBUKA ("Remember"), a Rwanda-based Tutsi survivors umbrella organization that includes 15 organizations in all. At one time IBUKA used to claim that the number of Tutsi survivors in 1994 was 300,000 persons; currently, IBUKA claims the number of Tutsi survivors was "nearer to 400,000."[96] Based on an estimated range of 500,000 to 600,000 Tutsi members of Rwanda's pre-April 1994 population (respectively, the estimate of GenoDynamics and of the 1991 Census), the range of Tutsi who perished in 1994 must have fallen somewhere between 100,000 and 200,000. Virtually every other Rwandan who perished at the time was Hutu.[97]

Table 1, column 4, "Hutu Deaths," depicts the likely ranges of Hutu deaths in the Rwandan genocide, based on a range of IBUKA estimates of Tutsi survivors of the April – July period, and assuming one of four estimates for the total deaths in Rwanda during the relevant period, introduced above.

Table 1. Ranges and ethnic compositions of deaths in the "Rwandan genocide" [1]

Total Deaths	Tutsi Survivors	Tutsi Deaths	Hutu Deaths
500,000	Between 300,000 and 400,000	Between 100,000 and 200,000	Between 300,000 and 400,000
800,000	Between 300,000 and 400,000	Between 100,000 and 200,000	Between 600,000 and 700,000
1,100,000	Between 300,000 and 400,000	Between 100,000 and 200,000	Between 900,000 and 1,000,000
2,000,000	Between 300,000 and 400,000	Between 100,000 and 200,000	Between 1.8 and 1.9 million

[1] With rounding, based on a Tutsi population in Rwanda of between approximately 500,000 and 600,000 at the start of April 1994, and based on a range for Tutsi survivors between 300,000 and 400,000 as of August 1994.

What we see here is that the smaller the total number of deaths, the greater the percentage comprised of Tutsi. Conversely, the greater the total number of deaths, the greater the number of Hutu deaths overall, and the greater the percentage comprised of Hutu. Based on an estimated range between 300,000 and 400,000 Tutsi survivors, if 500,000 Rwandans perished during April – July, then between 100,000 and 200,000 of them were Tutsi, and between 300,000 and 400,000 were Hutu. (See the second row.) Similarly, based on outlandish estimates such as that attributed to the Genocide Survivors Students Association of Rwanda, if 2 million Rwandans perished during April – July, then between 100,000 and 200,000 were Tutsi, and between 1.8 and 1.9 million were Hutu. (See the fifth row.) Small wonder, then, that the most devout advocates for the standard model denounce Davenport and Stam as "genocide deniers" at every opportunity, and have named them *persona non grata* in Rwanda. As the standard model holds that it was "mostly Tutsi" who perished in 1994, their work helps both to debunk and overturn the standard model.

Given that a larger—apparently substantially larger—death toll was suffered by Hutu, the "Rwandan genocide" commemorated in April 2014, based on the standard model, clearly had the most fundamental facts upside-down. But this, of course, points us to an alternative model for explaining Rwanda 1994—an alternative centered on a much different set of facts: That it was the RPF that stood to lose the most in the national elections called for in the Arusha Accords, and that the RPF resorted to military conquest of the country as the only way of guaranteeing that this would never happen. That it was the RPF that carried out the assassination of President Habyarimana, the event that triggered the mass killings. That at that moment, April 6, 1994, shortly before 8:30 PM local time, the RPF alone had prepared and mobilized its forces, and methodically swept across the country. That the RPF carried out major organized killings during the period (as distinct from "wilding"-type kill-or-be-killed murders and massacres at local levels, which were rampant and involved Hutu on Tutsi, Tutsi on Hutu, Hutu on Hutu, and Tutsi on Tutsi killings), a point attested to by the numbers above. And most telling of all, that in only 104 days, the RPF conquered Rwanda, where it still holds power today.

If the word *genocide* is to be applied to Rwanda 1994, should it not be applied to the principal organized perpetrators of the events of April-July—Paul Kagame and his Rwandan Patriotic Front? Should it not be recognized that the primary victims of his triumph were Hutu, whose earlier social revolution once led to the flight of many Tutsi, now triumphantly returned to minority power by the RPF and its U.S. and U.K. sponsors?

5. The West's alleged "failure to intervene"

During the month of April, 2014, permutations of the theme that the "international community looked away" while the "Rwandan genocide" took place was as best we can tell universal among both the political figures who spoke about it and the reporters and commentators who wrote about it for the establishment U.S. media. When the Security Council met on April 16 to discuss "Prevention and fight against genocide," Rwanda 1994 took center stage, virtually to the exclusion of any other mass killing. "As President Clinton has said many times, the failure of the United States to act during the 1994 genocide in Rwanda is his greatest regret," U.S. Ambassador Samantha Power said.[98] Speaking on the same occasion, Rwanda's Ambassador Eugène-Richard Gasana thanked UN Deputy Secretary-General Jan Eliasson for having "rallied the United Nations system to learn from its failure in Rwanda in 1994...."[99] In one form or another, speakers at this session of the Security Council made this point 19 different times.

This widely held belief has also been expressed by the White House's National Security Adviser Susan Rice, who claimed to be so "haunted" by the failure of the Clinton administration (at which time she was a staff member on its National Security Council) to intervene to stop the genocide, she "swore to herself that if [she] ever faced such a crisis again, [she] would come down on the side of dramatic action, going down in flames if that was required."[100]   Similarly, Samantha Power, back during her days at Harvard's Carr Center for Human Rights, wrote that "The Rwandan genocide proved to be the fastest, most efficient killing spree of the twentieth century. In 100 days, some 800,000 Tutsi and politically moderate Hutu were murdered. The United States did almost nothing to try to stop it....[T]he United States again stood on the sidelines."[101]   In its massive 1999 study of these events, Human Rights Watch even used the phrase "culpable passivity of 1994" to characterize the response of the "international community."[102]

But these are convenient falsehoods, even if repeated robotically now for 20 years. The fact of the matter is that the United States supported the RPF in its invasion of Rwanda from Uganda at least from October 1, 1990 onward; it trained Kagame, helped cover-up his and the RPF's serial crimes, including not only the initial invasion,[103] but also their killings of large numbers of Rwanda civilians over the next four years, and their shooting-down of Habyarimana's jet, the event which triggered the killings of the months that followed.

Knowing that Kagame's RPF had acquired military superiority over the FAR by 1993 if not earlier, the United States ran diplomatic interference for the RPF throughout 1993-1994, and has done so ever since. This included the support it gave the RPF as the latter used stalling tactics during the months leading up to the Habyarimana assassination, when the Arusha Accords called for power-sharing and the formation of the so-called Broad Based Transitional Government, plans that were terminated by the assassination and the RPF's military offensive. It also included support for the RPF's repeated rejections of ceasefires with the FAR from the second week after the assassination onward, when a strictly enforced ceasefire could have saved hundreds of thousands of lives;[104] and active backing of the RPF's final declaration that it is "categorically opposed to the proposed U.N. intervention force and will not under any circumstances cooperate in its setting up and operation,"[105] the actual policy position shared by the United States.

As Roméo Dallaire wrote in his memoir:

[T]he Americans put obstacle after obstacle in our way, with the British playing a coy supportive role. The French backed UN-

AMIR 2 but with conditions; the non-aligned countries were furious at the delays; and the RPF published a statement to the Security Council that looked very much like a manifesto against us, arguing that UNAMIR 2 was too late to stop the killing and could potentially destabilize the RPF's struggle for power. In fact, it was not too late; the massacres would continue for weeks. If I had been a suspicious soul, I could have drawn a link between the obstructive American position and the RPF's refusal to accept a sizeable UNAMIR 2.[106]

But UNAMIR 1's force commander didn't need to be a "suspicious soul" to draw these links—all that he or anyone needed is common sense and, crucially, not to be trapped inside the limited kind of group-think permitted by the standard model of the "Rwandan genocide." After all, as Dallaire acknowledged in his very next sentence: "In the pre-war period, the U.S. military attaché from the American embassy was observed going to [RPF headquarters in] Mulindi on a regular basis."[107] In short, the RPF and the United States had been reading from the same script from the very beginning. And though the end was now in sight—the United States would force Rwanda's interim government out of the United Nations by mid-July, and recognize the RPF as the legitimate government of Rwanda in late July 1994, within ten days of its declaration of victory over the FAR[108]—many innocent Rwandans would die before it was reached.

A State Department memo from September 1994 noted that the RPF "has engaged in a pattern of systematic killing of Hutu civilians...," and that the "purpose of the killing was a campaign of ethnic cleansing intended to clear certain areas in the south of Rwanda for Tutsi habitation." The "[RPF] and Tutsi civilian surrogates," the memo added, "had killed 10,000 or more Hutu civilian per month, with the [RPF] accounting for 95% of the killing."[109] Understandably, knowledge such as this has been suppressed from 1994 onward. Most important, it has not interfered at all with the ongoing U.S. support of the Kagame regime, and it has not haunted Susan Rice or Samantha Power. We believe that all of the belated regrets and apologies circulating widely around the date of the twentieth anniversary for an alleged U.S. or Western or UN "failure" to intervene in 1994 to stop the "Rwandan genocide" must be recognized for what they really were: Self-serving, hypocritical lies. The fact of the matter is that there *was* not just intervention from 1990 onward, but sponsorship and diplomatic and political protection of the RPF. And this real intervention was in support of the armed forces driving the real genocide— Paul Kagame and his RPF as they conquered the country and advanced perceived U.S. interests.

6. The ICTR delivers victor's justice

The ICTR was created by the UN Security Council in November 1994, only four months after the RPF had won its victory in Rwanda. It has served several strictly political objectives since then. But most important to understanding its operations, the ICTR was established to deliver "victor's justice" in relation to the events of 1994, by exclusively prosecuting the vanquished Hutu and finding them (largely) guilty of genocide and other major crimes, while shielding the RPF from prosecution. In so doing, the ICTR has helped Kagame to consolidate his dictatorial rule in Rwanda. Moreover, it has helped to justify Kagame's and his patrons' invasions and exploitation of the Democratic Republic of Congo (DRC), where the army of the new Rwanda has allegedly been hunting down the Hutu "*génocidaires*" of the old Rwanda, as his forces killed vast numbers from 1995 to the present.

Proof of the overwhelming political nature of the ICTR from its inception is provided, first, by the language of the Security Council Resolution that created this "international tribunal for the sole purpose of prosecuting persons responsible for genocide...."[110] Although the ICTY's trial and appeals chambers had to perform legal gymnastics to find Serbs guilty of genocide in the former Yugoslavia,[111] before the ICTR had even hired a chief prosecutor or a registrar, the factual truth of the Hutu genocide against Tutsi had been pronounced as given, negating any presumption of innocence. Indeed, in a decision handed down in June 2006, an ICTR appeals chamber ruled that the occurrence of genocide in Rwanda between April 6 and July 17, 1994 was a "fact of common knowledge" and therefore beyond challenge in court; thus the Hutu genocide against the

Tutsi became an "adjudicated fact," one that could never be argued before the ICTR again.[112] With this decision, the ICTR placed its seal on the official narrative of victimhood and villainy in the events of 1990-1994. As one critic responded sharply: This decision was "designed to prevent the defense from presenting the overwhelming evidence now developed that there were many complex reasons for the events in Rwanda, but genocide is not one of them. The political purpose is stated outright in the press release when the Tribunal state[d] that this decision by the Appeals Chamber should 'silence the rejectionist camp'."[113]

The ICTR's political nature is also seen in the fact that 100 percent of its 80 or so indictees have been Hutu, even though its Security Council mandate includes "serious violations of international and humanitarian law" committed between January 1 and December 31, 1994.[114] In fact, when the Security Council created the ICTR, the new RPF-led Rwandan government, which had inherited a seat on the Council from the interim government it had overthrown, was the only Council member to vote against the resolution (China abstained). Among the reasons that Manzi Bakuramutsa, the new RPF-led Rwanda's UN ambassador, gave after the no-vote, the one he stressed was the dates set for the jurisdiction of the ICTR. "My delegation," Bakuramutsa said, "proposed that account be taken of the period from 1 October 1990, the beginning of the war, to 17 July 1994, the end of the war."[115] Thus the new RPF-led Rwandan government wanted a tribunal that focused exclusively on the alleged Hutu genocide against Tutsi as far back as October 1990, but that cut-off its temporal jurisdiction in July 1994, immunizing the RPF for its slaughters of Hutu after it took power. Clearly, his government's fears were badly misplaced.

This culture of Tutsi and RPF impunity has remained an unbreakable rule at the ICTR. Filip Reyntjens, a Belgian academic and former investigator for the ICTR, recalls a conversation that he had with the ICTR's first chief prosecutor, Richard Goldstone, in July 1996. Reyntjens "asked Goldstone whether he intended to prosecute RPF suspects." Goldstone "answered with irritation that he did not see the need." Then Reyntjens "told him that there was compelling prima facie evidence that the RPF committed crimes within the Tribunal's mandate." Goldstone "replied that there was no such evidence."[116] The chief prosecutor's understanding that RPF crimes do not fall within the ICTR's mandate, even though they clearly do, and compelling evidence of RPF crimes exists, appears to have been operational from the beginning. And when the possibility of such prosecutions has been raised—as with Michael Hourigan's report to Louise Arbour on RPF responsibility for shooting-down Habyarimana's jet—such efforts were silenced and their authors quickly shown the door.

Another stunning example of the ICTR's political nature can be found in its most egregious case of extracting guilty pleas at a time early in its history when the defendants were poorly represented and essentially defenseless. Jean Kambanda had served as prime minister in the interim government from April 9, 1994, until the interim government fled the country in July. He was arrested in Nairobi in July 1997, then held for an extended period of time in Dodoma, Tanzania, rather than at the tribunal's official detention facility in Arusha, where the prosecution kept him under guard, without access to a defense counsel, and visited only by prosecutors and interrogators. Kambanda claims that during this period, he was tortured; most certainly he lived a vulnerable existence under great duress. "The transcript of Kambanda's interrogation, based on sixty hours of interviews, is an extraordinary document," Linda Melvern writes, suppressing what really made it extraordinary. "It gives unprecedented insight into how the genocide was perpetrated."[117] On the contrary, it gives unprecedented insight into a prosecution that wanted one of its "Big Fish" defendants to cop a plea of genocide, no matter what measures were required to extract it.

Although Kambanda was convicted of "conspiracy to commit genocide,"[118] nowhere in his actual guilty plea of April 28, 1998 did he admit to a conspiracy at any time, and notably not one organized *before* the killings started on April 7, 1994, and hence relevant to proving a planned genocide. At most, "Jean Kambanda admits there was in Rwanda in 1994 a widespread and systematic attack against the civilian population of Tutsi, the purpose of which was to exterminate them," the plea asserts, but it asserts nothing to the effect that he himself was engaged in such activities. The plea also asserts that Kambanda was the prime minister of the interim government, exercising *de jure* authority.[119]

Before his guilty plea was filed, Kambanda had requested representation by his lawyer, the Belgian Johan Scheers. The prosecution denied his request. Instead, Kambanda was held in isolation until the end of April 1998, when "he was brought to enter a guilty plea after being convinced by his [prosecution-imposed] lawyer Michael Oliver Inglis, acting in league with his personal friend and former partner in a law practice, Deputy Prosecutor [Bernard] Muna, that he would get away with a light sentence."[120] It is not difficult to understand the machinations that went into extracting Kambanda's plea. In September 1998, the trial chamber accepted his plea, convicted him on multiple counts including "conspiracy to commit genocide," and sentenced him to life in prison.[121] This, an approving Linda Melvern writes, was how "Jean Kambanda entered the history books, the first person ever to plead guilty to the crime of genocide at an international court hearing."[122]

Chief Prosecutor Louise Arbour issued a statement: "The sentencing of Jean Kambanda and the conviction of Jean-Paul Akayesu [two days earlier] are the most significant steps to date in the eradication of the culture of impunity in Rwanda and elsewhere in the world."[123] But Kambanda renounced his guilty plea immediately after his conviction, citing numerous dirty tricks by the prosecutor and his attorney. As John Laughland observed: "So the landmark conviction of a former head of government for genocide by an international tribunal—a conviction which was itself used to obtain guilty verdicts in subsequent trials—was in fact made on a rather confused man who immediately rescinded his guilty plea, on the basis that it had been made under duress, out of concern for his family's safety, and following bad advice from a lawyer who was an old friend of the prosecutor and whom he had not instructed."[124]

Meanwhile, the real culture of RPF impunity (which Arbour helped to preserve during her tenure as chief prosecutor at the ICTR) remains perfectly intact. When Carla Del Ponte, Arbour's successor as chief prosecutor, attempted to bring indictments against some RPF members, she not only failed, she was ousted from the ICTR for her effort.[125] Del Ponte announced in April 2002 that her office had "opened investigations into three massacres." She also "showed [Kagame] a list of massacres we will be investigating."[126] Kagame promised her his cooperation. But instead the flow of Tutsi witnesses on which the prosecution relied to conduct its cases was turned off in Kigali, forcing the postponement of trials;[127] in perfect character, RPF officials started denouncing Del Ponte for "genocide denial," "divisionism," "revisionism," and the like. In the summer of 2002, Del Ponte informed the Security Council that the ICTR had ceased functioning.[128] By the spring of 2003, the United States and Britain were pressuring Kofi Annan to remove Del Ponte as chief prosecutor when her mandate expired that September. On May 15, Del Ponte met twice with Pierre Joseph Prosper, the Bush administration's ambassador-at-large for war crimes. During their second encounter, at the Washington residence of the Swiss ambassador to the United States, Prosper informed her that "some states think that the [ICTR] should have its own prosecutor. You will not be reappointed."[129]

In a July 29 letter that Annan sent to the President of the Security Council, Annan stated that he had "consulted with the members of the Security Council regarding the appointment of the Prosecutor. In the light of those consultations, I have formed the view that it is now time to split the positions of Prosecutor of the [ICTY] and the Prosecutor of the [ICTR], so that they are occupied by different people."[130] In a perfunctory session of the Security Council on August 28, a U.S.-sponsored resolution was adopted that for the first time in the histories of the ICTR and ICTY, split their common chief prosecutor into two different chief prosecutors.[131] Del Ponte's willingness to investigate RPF crimes had gotten her fired.[132]

Annan replaced Del Ponte with the Gambian jurist, Hassan B. Jallow, a committed agent of the United States and Britain and, by the same token, acceptable to Kagame. Now, 11 years later, Jallow has maintained the ICTR's perfect record of never indicting a member of the RPF. Responding to years of criticisms of the prosecution's selective and discriminatory practice of indicting Hutus but never members of the RPF,[133] Jallow wrote in 2005:

> The issue of judicial control of the prosecutorial discretion has arisen in the context of allegations of 'selective' prosecution by the [prosecution]. It will be recalled that the Rwandan genocide was directed at the elimination of the Tutsi minority and the moderate Hutus by the majority Hutu in government. Opposing the Hutu government of the day was the Rwandan Patriotic Front..., which waged a war of liberation and defeated the Hutu government of the day, putting an end to the genocide. There

42

are allegations that in the course of the war, fought alongside the genocide, the RPF had itself committed atrocities.[134]

But no matter: The ICTR is by its "very nature" an "ad hoc Tribunal," Jallow explained, and it was "meant to deal with one situation....The Statute of the Tribunal itself does not require the prosecution of *all* offenders."[135]   Sure enough, in its stream of indictments of official Hutu enemy targets, and in its incapacity or refusal to indict a single member of the RPF, even when one of its chief prosecutors tried to bring indictments, the ICTR has achieved true "victor's justice," and perfected the culture of RPF impunity.   In recounting how, at the so-called *ad hoc* tribunals, "[U.S.] foreign policy trumps international justice," Robin Philpot points out that David Scheffer, the "first United States Ambassador-at-Large for War Crime issues," confessed as regards the Yugoslavia Tribunal: "By [1999], the tribunal was a potent judicial tool, and I had enough support...in Washington to wield it like a battering ram in the execution of U.S. and NATO policy."[136]   Had Hassan Jallow been honest about his tenure at the ICTR, he would have dropped the disguise of "prosecutorial discretion," and made the same confession.

7. The alleged Hutu "conspiracy to commit genocide" that never was [137]

In stating matter-of-factly that the "Rwandan genocide was directed at the elimination of the Tutsi minority and the moderate Hutus by the majority Hutu in government," Hassan Jallow was repeating what is, unquestionably, the core belief concerning events in Rwanda 1994.

"Overwhelming evidence indicates that the extermination of Tutsis by Hutus had been planned months in advance of its actual execution," the Final Report of the UN Commission of Experts stated in late 1994.[138] Indeed, Hutu-based genocidal planning has also been a premise of every indictment that has ever been brought by the prosecution at the ICTR. Thus, the indictment of Army Col. Théoneste Bagosora and three other Hutu military figures stated that "From late July 1990 until July 1994, [they] conspired among themselves and with others to work out a plan

43

with the intent to exterminate the civilian Tutsi population...."[139] In
Daniel Jonah Goldhagen's words, "[T]he assassination of Hutu President
Juvénal Habyarimana (likely perpetrated by Hutu members of his own
movement) was the spectacular event blamed on the Tutsi, and the pretext
for the exterminationist leadership of the governing National Republican
Movement for Democracy to put into action plans long germinating for
the 'final solution' to their Tutsi problem."[140]

We regard this belief in the existence of a Hutu "conspiracy to commit
genocide" against the Tutsi to be the *foundational lie* in the standard
model's claim of a "Rwandan genocide,"[141] the truth of which has been
institutionalized and disseminated by the United Nations, by "Friends of
the New Rwanda" (governments and private sector supporters of Rwanda
under RPF rule[142]), by legions of academics, Rwanda specialists,
Kagame-Power enthusiasts, human rights organizations, the establishment news media, a famous Hollywood film, the prosecution at the ICTR,
and, at least in the early years, by the ICTR's trial and appeals chambers
as well.

In Sections 2 - 6, we have shown that this core belief is incompatible
with massive and compelling evidence on the issue. Most important, the
evidence shows that Kagame's RPF was responsible for the event that
"triggered" the killings (the Habyarimama assassination); that it was
ready for action on April 6 and was the only effective military force in
Rwanda before and during the surge of mass killings, as the RPF quickly
conquered the country. And we have shown that the numbers and ethnic
composition of Rwanda's dead do not support standard model claims; on
the contrary, the evidence shows that Hutu deaths far exceeded deaths of
Tutsi.

Each of these counter-points provides powerful and compelling reasons
to believe that the standard model of the "Rwandan genocide" is completely false, reversing the locus of the primary killers and victims in the
foundational lie.

But yet another compelling reason to reject the Hutu plan-lie derives
from an unexpected source: namely, the ICTR itself. This is because,
whether in the trial or the appeals chambers, the ICTR's judges have consistently acquitted on this charge, or reversed convictions on appeal. We
find this to be a remarkable turn of events, because as we have seen, the

ICTR *is* a politicized body that never prosecutes anybody but Hutu, and that regularly finds Hutu guilty of participating in a genocide—the pre-ordained premise of the ICTR—but not of a conspiracy to commit one.

As we noted, in the indictment of Bagosora *et al.* (i.e., "From late July 1990 until July 1994..."), a Hutu "conspiracy to commit genocide" refers to one that existed some time *prior* to April 6, 1994, so that once the assassination of Habyarimana had been carried out, the Hutu conspirators could also carry out their *plan* to exterminate the Tutsi.

But it is precisely this notion of a Hutu "conspiracy to commit genocide" that the ICTR's own judges have consistently rejected. We reviewed the trial judgments as well as the judgments on appeal of what to date have been the 15 most important cases argued before the ICTR.[143] In all 15 of these judgments (the sixteenth defendant, Joseph Nzirorera, died in custody prior to the end of his trial), the defendants were either acquitted of the charge in the trial judgment, or previous convictions were reversed on appeal. Especially given the pro-Kagame and anti-Hutu political role and bias of the ICTR, this alone is a compelling refutation of the Hutu "conspiracy to commit genocide." (See "Appendix I" for a discussion of specific ICTR cases and judgments on this charge.)

But then how could a lie as big as the Hutu "conspiracy to commit genocide" have ever been institutionalized in the first place, given the wide array of incompatible facts of the kind that we have outlined? One crucial factor is that the United States and Britain, with their great economic, political and communications power, and influence over the UN, were the co-conspirators with the RPF and Kagame, first in invading and conquering Rwanda, and then invading the Democratic Republic of Congo. This Great Power support, combined with the public's and the media's distance from and unfamiliarity with central African affairs, made the construction and dissemination of false propaganda on Rwanda very easy. And it has been almost miraculous in turning the truth on its head.

Also important in institutionalizing this foundational lie is the fact that organizations such as African Rights and Human Rights Watch, advocates for the Hutu "conspiracy to commit genocide" claim since 1994, published extensive dossiers of killings carried out by the FAR and Hutu individuals and groups. African Rights amassed 750 pages of gory detail (eventually expanded to over 1200), setting the scene for everything that followed.[144] Human Rights Watch's focus on Hutu actions in one prefecture, Butare, in the country's south, runs 163 pages and reads like a brief drafted at the behest of the ICTR's chief prosecutor.[145] Such riches of dramatic detail convey the impression that each violent event must be taken as an instance of something far more encompassing—"The Genocide."

But given the considerably greater number of Hutu than Tutsi victims in 1994, it surely would have been possible for these and other chroniclers to assemble comparable or even greater detail suggesting an RPF genocidal plan and the bloody consequences that followed from it. Instead, the human rights activists and journalists who were covering Rwanda followed the political line that flowed from their government's interest in the outcome, which seems to have been mentally pre-programmed in them to interpret and report about events in only one Kagame-friendly framework. The UN also followed this party-line, and when its researchers like Robert Gersony came up with detailed evidence of RPF mass killings, it quashed the evidence.[146] These institutionalized biases led the UN, human rights groups and journalists to one conclusion only, just as the same biases continue to lead them to the same erroneous conclusion, 20 years later.[147]

Over many years ICTR jurisprudence on this issue has come around to a position that, in rejecting the "conspiracy to commit genocide" charge based on the lack of supportive evidence, is closer to that of so-called "genocide deniers" and "revisionists" than its advocates are willing to admit. As the French journalist Thierry Cruvellier wrote in 2011, after the appeals chamber in the Military I cases had demolished the conspiracy model even further than had the trial chamber in 2008: "In 300 pages, it slashed the trial judgment so deeply that, 17 years after the court was created, it seems almost impossible to understand what's the narrative that has come out of the most important trial at the ICTR."[148] His suggestion, which we do not accept, is that "There was a genocide…but it was brainless." On the contrary, we believe that there *was* in fact a genocide in Rwanda in 1994—but its brain was the RPF, Paul Kagame, and their supportive U.S. and U.K. officials.

8. Did Paul Kagame's RPF really "stop the genocide"?

It is widely believed, and a core component of the standard model, that the "Rwandan genocide" came to an end only when the RPF drove the "Hutu Power extremists," the Rwandan Armed Forces, the Gendarmerie, the Presidential Guard, the Para-Commando unit, and the Interahamwe and Impuzamugambi from the country into exile. "The organizers [of the genocide] used the slaughter of Tutsi to draw the RPF into renewed combat," we read in Human Rights Watch's version of the events. In response, "The RPF resumed the war in part to stop the massacres...."[149] "The mass killing in Rwanda was brought to an end in July, and earlier in the eastern part of the country," African Rights reported as early as September 1994. "The credit for this lies with the RPF, whose military advance was the chief reason the killings were halted. The RPF was not responsible for the genocide; moreover it was largely responsible for halting the genocide."[150] Asked by the French newspaper *Libération* whether he was "still at war, 20 years after the genocide?" Kagame's reply could have been drawn from either the Human Rights Watch or the African Rights reports: "We waged war back in 1994, when we stopped the genocide."[151]

But this view is completely incompatible with the serious evidence we have already discussed. The driving force for the mass killings that began on April 7, 1994, and rapidly escalated, was the RPF brain-trust, led by Kagame, whose one and only road to power was by violence that was long planned, highly efficient, and eminently successful. That is, Kagame-RPF violence was *proactive*, not reactive. Kagame-RPF rejections of FAR ceasefire offers were *strategic*, not poor diplomacy.

The same is true for the Kagame-RPF's rejection of the FAR's unconditional surrender offer. Dallaire recounts delivering this offer to the RPF. They "dismissed it outright," he writes. "Once more they were going for the extremists' [*sic*] jugular. The [FAR] insisted on a ceasefire so they could redeploy forces to stop the killings. The RPF insisted that the killings had to stop before they would agree to a ceasefire."[152] Similarly, Kagame-RPF warnings both to Dallaire in Rwanda and at the United Nations in New York City that if the UN placed additional UNAMIR troops on the ground, they would regard these troops as enemy combatants and fight them as well as the FAR, weren't empty threats—they were deadly *serious* threats.[153]

In all of this, the Kagame-RPF were aided and abetted by U.S., British, and UN officials, who manifestly were not standing idly-by and doing nothing in 1994, but were actively engaged in supporting the Kagame-RPF conquest of Rwanda. And since conquering Rwanda was the Kagame-RPF's desideratum from 1990 onward, the Kagame-RPF neither "stopped the genocide" nor permitted any other force to try and stop the mass killings of Hutu and Tutsi until they had completed their conquest—after which date, the Kagame-RPF went right on killing Hutu, first within Rwanda itself, later within the eastern Democratic Republic of Congo (formerly Zaire).

That Kagame and the RPF were the principal organized killers in Rwanda 1994, as shown by their rejection of the Arusha terms, by the number and composition of deaths, and by their refusal to negotiate before and during the peak killing period. Indeed, it would be more accurate to state that the Kagame-RPF have never stopped their genocide against Hutu, even if at times, they have put it on hold.

As Filip Reyntjens has written, the "RPF behaves similarly to an occupying force, and it is seen as such by many Rwandans, who resist in a way reminiscent of the situation in occupied France during World War II."[154] With the conquest of Rwanda and the establishment of a genuine dictatorship by his ethnic minority group, and even more specifically, by his military elite, Kagame Power flourishes.

9. "Africa's World War": Kagame's alleged pursuit of *"génocidaires"* in Zaire—the Democratic Republic of Congo—and the deaths of millions[155]

The Kagame-RPF conquest of Rwanda was followed two years later by an invasion of the very large central African country now known as the Democratic Republic of Congo (the DRC, which had been known as the Democratic Republic of Zaire through May 1997).[156] Launched in September 1996 under several layers of pretext, this war has continued in fits-and-starts up to the present day, with the collaboration of Uganda,

Map of Zaire – The Democratic Republic of Congo, derived from EZILON MAPS

Burundi, and the United States and its close allies, notably Canada and the United Kingdom.

The large number of armed combatants, the monumental bloodshed, death toll, and human catastrophe suffered by the native population and mass of Hutu refugees in the DRC is on a scale so great that it has been referred to as "Africa's first World War," [157] the "greatest humanitarian crisis in the world today [*ca.* 2005],"[158] and as the "world's deadliest crisis since World War II."[159]

The numbers of victims of the continuing Kagame-led assault have been immense. A UN report of October 2002 cited an estimate that "more than 3.5 million excess deaths" had occurred in the DRC between August 1998 and September 2002; the report concluded that "These deaths are a direct result of the occupation by Rwanda and Uganda."[160] A mortality study published in January 2009 estimated the "excess death toll in DR Congo since 1998 to be 5.4 million, of which 4.6 million occurred in the five insecure eastern provinces"[161]—North Kivu and South Kivu in particular, exactly where Kagame's footprint had made its deepest impression. Perhaps most important, the October 2010 UN "Mapping Exercise" of the "most serious" crimes in the DRC claimed that the RPF and its proxy forces had carried out "systematic and widespread attacks…which targeted very large numbers of Rwanda Hutu refugees and members of the Hutu civilian population, resulting in their death." These attacks, the report continues, "reveal a number of damning elements that, if they were proven before a competent court, could be classified crimes of genocide."[162] Undeniably, we are dealing here with mass killing on a scale far exceeding that of Rwanda 1994, and reaching levels not seen since the World War II era.

The October 1993 coup carried out by the Tutsi-dominated military in Burundi and the interethnic conflicts that followed led to as many as 50,000 deaths. The military had accused the FRODEBU party of the assassinated Hutu President Melchior Ndadaye of having planned to commit genocide against Burundi's Tutsi minority—hence its need to pre-empt FRODEBU's alleged plans. By March 1994, some 260,000 Burundian Hutu refugees remained in camps in neighboring Rwanda, and as many as 55,000 in Zaire.[163] By the completion of the RPF's final offensive in Rwanda in 1994, and the RPF's pogroms and ethnic cleansing operations in the months that followed, an estimated 2,257,000 Rwandans had fled their country, with perhaps as many as 1.5 million Hutu refugees having fled west to Zaire, another 626,000 east to Tanzania, 278,000 south to Burundi, and 97,000 north to Uganda.[164] Included within this massive refugee flow were no doubt members of the Rwandan armed forces that had been overthrown by Kagame's RPF, but there were far larger numbers of Hutu civilians. As a consequence of these recurring armed conflicts in Burundi and Rwanda, the situation in the eastern Zairean provinces of North Kivu, South Kivu, and Orientale Province was economically, politically, and socially unstable; and given the fact that the government of Mobutu Sese Seko was in Kinshasa, at the opposite end of the country, the Zairean government was largely absent from these eastern provinces.

According to the standard model of the "Rwandan genocide" and its aftermath, it was the threat posed to the new RPF-controlled Rwanda and to the stability of the Great Lakes Region in central Africa by the presence of these Hutu "*génocidaires*" in eastern Zaire that left the armed forces of Rwanda, Uganda, and Burundi no choice but to invade Zaire to clean them out. Adam Jones, a "genocide" studies professor at the University of British Columbia, quotes approvingly from Michela Wrong's 2001 book, *In the Footsteps of Mr. Kurtz*, where she writes that "Like a monstrous cancer, the [Hutu refugee] camps coalesced, solidified and implanted themselves in the flesh of east Zaire."[165] Jones himself writes that "Hutu extremists inflicted genocidal atrocities against Tutsi living in eastern Zaire and staged cross-border raids into Rwanda, prompting the newly installed RPF regime in Rwanda to launch operations in the region that themselves led to the deaths of thousands of civilians, together with hardcore *génocidaires*."[166] And Jones goes on to quote approvingly Christian Scherrer, a professor of Peace Studies at the Hiroshima Peace Institute, who has written: "The export of genocide from Rwanda is the main cause in the spread of conflict to the whole of the Central African region, and the chief reason for the unprecedented violence, intensity, and destructiveness of that conflict."[167]

In Jones's, Scherrer's, and Wrong's view, the Hutu refugees carried "The Genocide" with them into eastern Zaire in 1994 (because it was *inside of them*, a *part of them*), where it then metastasized and spread to the whole of central Africa, eventually leading to the wars and mass killings that followed.

But, in fact, the truth is quite the opposite: It was Kagame's Rwandan Patriotic Army (RPA, the new name of the national army of Rwanda after the RPF took power) that literally exported their 1990 invasion of Rwanda and their 46 month war against Rwanda's Hutu from Rwanda to eastern Zaire in 1996, and then beyond.[168]

By the spring and summer of 1996, Kagame-friendly media in Rwanda had already begun to publish threats against the Mobutu regime, accusing Mobutu of threatening Rwanda, and even framing the situation in eastern

Zaire as a "genocide under incubation" against the region's Tutsi population.[169] Just as the RPF's advances and slaughters in Rwanda 1994 had
allegedly been in response to the Hutu "genocide" against that country's
Tutsi population, so the long-planned invasion, occupation, mass killings,
and resource exploitation in eastern Zaire were to be justified as a pre-
emptive war to prevent the next alleged "genocide" against the Tutsi from
occurring. Filip Reyntjens writes that Yoweri Museveni, Uganda's long-
time dictator, is on record stating that "as early as 1995, Kagame had re-
cruited 2000 Zairean Tutsi...into the RPA with a view of carrying out
military action against the refugee camps;" more recruits were added
later.[170] Having infiltrated South Kivu province along the border with
Rwanda and Burundi, and then become operational at the start of September 1996, this Tutsi "rebellion" was in reality the "spearhead of a fifth
column," as Roland Pourtier put it. "The strategic choice [of Kigali] to
attack the camps clearly shows the fundamental objectives of a 'rebellion'
that was no longer [a rebellion], because what really happened was the
extension of the Rwandan civil war [*sic*] into Zairean territory."[171]

Over the next nine months in eastern Zaire, one Hutu refugee camp after
another came under attack. Rwandan, Ugandan, and Burundian armed
forces participated in these attacks, as did multiple proxy forces, most notably the *Alliance des forces Démocratiques pour la libération du Congo-
Zaire* (AFDL), the lead "rebel" faction, but one that did not even exist
until the month of October, after the attacks on eastern Zaire had begun.
The United States also participated in these cross-border assaults. Both
the invading armies and their proxies received steady U.S. supplies, reconnaissance, communications, and transportation support, as well as
diplomatic cover, no matter how many people were killed.[172] Gérard
Prunier describes how "Washington operated a multi-purpose anti-Mobutu
machine which ranged from the half-humanitarian, half-military support
given by the International Rescue Committee, long rumored to have been
an NGO close to sensitive segments of the U.S. administration, to the
soothing testimony given on the question of the missing [Hutu] refugees
by Assistance Secretary of State...Phyllis Oakley in December 1996."[173]
Reyntjens concludes that the "United States was aware of the intentions
of Kagame to attack the refugee camps and probably assisted him in doing
so. In addition, they deliberately lied about the number and fate of the

refugees remaining in Zaire, in order to avoid the deployment of an international humanitarian force, which could have saved tens of thousands of human lives, but which was resented by Kigali and the AFDL."[174] This pattern is perfectly familiar, as we've observed in several sections above.

On May 16, 1997, Mobutu fled Kinshasa for his hometown of Gbadolite, at the far northern end of Zaire, and then to France; he died four months later, an exile in Morocco. On May 17, Kinshasa was officially in the possession of the RPA and the AFDL, whose latecomer leader, Laurent-Désiré Kabila, was sworn-in as president on May 29. As Kagame told the *Washington Post* in a July 1997 interview, "As long as the people at the forefront were Zairean, the rebellion [*sic*] was going to be easy."[175]

During this first phase of the Rwandan-Ugandan wars on Zaire-DRC, an estimated 200,000 to 246,000 Rwandan Hutu refugees are believed to have died.[176] And the 1996-1997 phase was minor in comparison with the major war that Rwanda and Uganda restarted in August 1998, the effects from which central Africa is still reeling today (as reflected in the death tolls reported above).[177]

This terrible, criminal treatment of the Hutu refugees was based on both local and foreign interests. The RPF conquerors of Rwanda were not happy at the prospect of a return to Rwanda of large numbers of Hutu refugees, who would not be friendly to the new Tutsi regime, and very well might have tried to re-occupy land and properties often taken over by Tutsi. Honoré N'Gbanda, a former security adviser to Mobutu, was quite categorical about this: "Kagame did not want the Hutu back in Rwanda."[178] Leon Kengo, a former prime minister of Zaire, gave one reason why: "[Kagame] wanted them to return to Rwanda as stragglers, one by one, at his mercy. The international community just let him do as he liked."[179]

Rwandan and allied interest in exploiting the resources of the DRC also demanded an excuse for invasion and occupation, and a primary and apparently saleable one has been the alleged need to clean-out the Hutu *"génocidaires."* As long as the *Armée pour la Libération du Rwanda* (ALIR) and later the *Forces Démocratiques de Libération du Rwanda* (FDLR), the two main Hutu-based anti-Kagame fighting forces in the eastern Zaire-DRC, remained armed, the RPA would always have a pretext to invade.

U.S. and U.K. interest in the treatment of the refugees was closely related to the basis of their support for Kagame and the RPA: The latter were tacit agents of a program to enlarge U.S. power in central Africa, displacing the French, replacing Habyarimana with Kagame, Mobutu with the AFDL-Kabila front, and thereby allowing a more unobstructed exploitation of this resource-rich area of the planet.[180] Just as the mass killings in Rwanda were acceptable "collateral damage" of the earlier drive for power, so were the slaughters of large numbers in the eastern Zaire-DRC.

It must be stressed that the prime killer here was Paul Kagame, whose toll of victims, first in Rwanda and then in Zaire-DRC, runs into the millions, and surely exceeds that of Idi Amin by a factor of at least five.[181] And yet, in one of the miracles of modern propaganda, Kagame became a savior-modernizer-moral giant for the U.S., U.K., and Canadian establishment to admire (and exploit). But surely this favorable portrayal of Kagame flows from the fact that he served U.S. and other powerful interests in clearing out adversarial regimes that were under strong French influence (Habyarimana's and Mobutu's), assuring U.S. dominance in the Great Lakes region, and easier access to its resources. U.S., British, and Canadian support of Kagame's mass killings has been steady throughout, even if sometimes embarrassing. This extended naturally to the UN, which was unable to provide effective aid to the very large numbers of refugees under relentless attack by Kagame and his allies, who shelled them, bombed them, assaulted them on the ground, and starved them and drove their members, including large numbers of women and children, into the jungles of Zaire-DRC.

On November 9, 1996, with the Hutu refugees in eastern Zaire in serious trouble, and following a wave of publicity and strong pressure on the Security Council to act, the Council did pass the Canadian-sponsored Resolution 1078, calling for an "immediate ceasefire," the "voluntary repatriation of refugees to their country of origin," the creation of a "multinational force...for humanitarian purposes in eastern Zaire," and the establishment of "humanitarian corridors" for the delivery of assistance.[182] This in turn was followed on November 15 by Resolution 1080, which explicitly authorized the "establishment for humanitarian purposes of a temporary multinational force" under Chapter VII of the UN

Charter.[183]

But the very day the Council adopted this second resolution, Kagame's forces attacked the Mugunga refugee camp, west of Goma, a large city in North Kivu, along Zaire's border with Rwanda. As this RPA attack was launched from west-to-east, toward Rwanda, its purpose clearly was to force the involuntary repatriation of as many Hutu refugees back to Rwanda as quickly as possible, and then to claim that the refugee crisis had been resolved.

Immediately, as if on-cue, U.S., British, and Canadian political and military figures began expressing doubts about whether the multinational force called for by the two resolutions was still necessary. The Canadian General Maurice Baril, who had been designated the force commander for the still unmanned force, agreed that the repatriation was well underway and that the multinational force was not needed. Subsequently, the Canadian Raymond Chrétien, the Secretary-General's special envoy on the crisis, briefed the UN in New York City on December 13, at which time he stated that the "usefulness" of the "multinational force will decrease," even though, as Reyntjens notes, a week earlier Chrétien had stated that the "humanitarian force is indispensible." In short, although a propaganda campaign had been undertaken to make it seem like a multinational force would be deployed to eastern Zaire, one was "never seriously considered"[184] and the U.S., Britain, and Canada never would have permitted it.

In 2002, Robin Philpot interviewed Chrétien at the Canadian Embassy in Paris. Asked about the multinational force for Zaire that never was, Chrétien admitted that "there was no political will to deploy the multinational force," and that the failure to create one had left "A million people dead!"[185]

But this was what the Abe Lincoln of the New Africa and Bill Clinton of the old United States wanted back in 1996. It also repeats the pattern of the withdrawal of UN troops from Rwanda in the spring of 1994, when Kagame and Clinton wanted to clear the path for the RPF's final offensive—at the cost of facilitating the *earlier* "genocide."

10. The apocryphal "Genocide Fax"

As we have shown, evidence of a longstanding Hutu plan to commit genocide against the Tutsi of Rwanda is non-existent, although the "conspiracy" charge has been trumpeted in establishment Western circles for at least the past 21 years.[186] Robin Philpot points out that in September 1994, shortly after Roméo Dallaire had left his post as UNAMIR force commander and returned to Canada, Dallaire "took part in an important French-language television program in Montréal." During the program, someone asked Dallaire for his thoughts about the alleged plan to "exterminate Tutsis." Correcting the questioner, Dallaire replied: "The plan was more political. The aim was to eliminate the coalition of moderates....I think that the excesses that we saw were beyond people's ability to plan and organize. There was a process to destroy the political elements in the moderate camp. There was a breakdown and hysteria absolutely....But nobody could have foreseen or planned the magnitude of the destruction we saw."[187]

For Philpot, the significance of Dallaire's September, 1994 dismissal of the standard model of the "Rwandan genocide" (i.e., "nobody could have foreseen or planned...") is that this early Dallaire, fresh out of UNAMIR, contradicts how the Dallaire of later years would come to speak and write about Rwanda 1994. Some more-or-less credible, additional evidence of Hutu planning was therefore very much needed—and lo-and-behold, in November 1995, it was suddenly provided in the form of the "Genocide Fax."

On November 26, 1995, *The Observer* (London) published a report titled "UN Suppressed Warning of Rwanda Genocide Plan." Based on an investigation by the Belgium newspaper *De Morgen*, *The Observer* reported that "A secret cable reveals that senior officials at the United Nations were warned three months before last year's genocide that Hutu extremists were planning to 'exterminate' the minority Tutsis in Rwanda. The subsequent slaughter, spearheaded by the Interahamwe, only stopped when RPF rebels overthrew the former government forces three months later."[188]

As best we can tell, this is the very first public record in the English language of what has come to be known as the "Genocide Fax." If authentic, it would provide some documentary evidence of early United Nations knowledge of Hutu planning to "exterminate" Tutsi. Dated January 11, 1994, this two-page fax was allegedly sent over an encrypted phone line by UNAMIR Force Commander Lieut.-Gen. Roméo Dallaire from his headquarters in Kigali to the Canadian Gen. Maurice Baril at the UN Department of Peacekeeping Operations (DPKO) in New York City. (For our analysis of the "Genocide Fax" based on the different extant copies of the document that have been in circulation since November 27, 1995, see "Appendix II.")

Titled "Request for Protection for Informant,"[189] Dallaire reported that UNAMIR had met with a "top level trainer in the cadres of Interhamwe-[*sic*] armed militia of MRND...."[190] Dallaire added that the informant—who later was identified as Jean-Pierre Turatsinze—told UNAMIR that he knew the location of an MRND "weapons cache with at least 135 weapons," and that he would be willing to take UNAMIR to that cache "tonight" if UNAMIR guaranteed "that he and his family...be placed under [UNAMIR] protection." "It is our intention to take action within the next 36 hours," Dallaire informed the DPKO.

But what makes this the "*Genocide* Fax" are two paragraphs numbered 6 and 7 in which it states that the informant "has been ordered to register all Tutsi in Kigali. He suspects it is for their extermination. Example he gave was that in 20 minutes his personnel could kill up to 1000 Tutsis" (para. 6). "Informant states he disagrees with anti-Tutsi extermination," we read in the next paragraph, and that the "President does not have full control over all elements of his old party/faction" (para. 7).

"I was silent," Dallaire writes in his 2003 memoir, "hit by the depth and reality of this information. It was as if the informant Jean-Pierre had opened the floodgates on the hidden world of the extremist third force, which until this point had been a presence we could sense but couldn't grasp." [191]

Both Philip Gourevitch and Human Rights Watch's Alison Des Forges were early and eager promoters of the "Genocide Fax." The fax "reported in startling detail the preparations that were underway to carry out...an extermination program," Gourevitch wrote in *The New Yorker*. "As it happened, everything Dallaire's informant told him came true three months later."[192] In its massive *"Leave None to Tell the Story"*, Human

Rights Watch reported that Dallaire had written: "Informant states that he disagrees with anti-Tutsi extermination"[193]—as we have just seen, extermination being the central theme of the "Genocide Fax."

Fortunately, Michael Dobbs has posted a copy of the DPKO's response to Dallaire at the website of the National Security Archive.[194] Also dated January 11, 1994, it is striking that nowhere does this response indicate any awareness of the paragraphs 6 and 7's *"anti-Tutsi extermination"* theme. Instead, the DPKO discussed the need for UNAMIR to maintain Kigali as a "weapons-secure area" as provided for in the Arusha Peace Agreement, as well as indicating what additional steps Dallaire should take, if he is "convinced that the information provided by the informant is absolutely reliable...." But the DPKO response is silent on the imminent genocide theme.

Why would the DPKO in New York City fail to take any notice at all of the most grave allegations the "Genocide Fax" supposedly made about Hutu plans to exterminate Tutsi ("anti-Tutsi extermination")?

We believe that there is a simple explanation for this discrepancy: The so-called "Genocide Fax," as it exists today in the official records related to Rwanda 1994, is a *counterfeit.*

So where did the counterfeit "Genocide Fax" come from?

In early November 1995, Kigali played host to an international conference titled "Genocide, Impunity, and Accountability: Dialogue for a National and International Response."[195] One hundred sixty-five people participated in the conference, some 58 of whom came from other countries. A recurring theme at the conference was the failure of certain states (e.g., Belgium and France), and of the United Nations especially, to act on intelligence that they allegedly possessed about Hutu plans to exterminate Tutsi. In response, Shaharyar Khan, the Secretary-General's Special Representative for Rwanda since July 1994, initiated a review of the UN's files on Rwanda for the relevant period of the UN mission: October 1993 through March 1994. Twelve days later, the Khan review "confirm[ed] the view that there was no information or indication of planned genocide. There were, of course, warnings of armed clashes, violence and killings on an ethnic basis."[196] A chronology of the potentially most relevant UN documents that had been reviewed listed the following summary for a document dated January 11, 1994: "Informant provided infor-

mation of plans by Interhamwe [*sic*] to disrupt process and assassinate
moderates. FC [Force Commander Dallaire] instructed by us to approach
President [Habyarimana] and inform diplomatic community."[197] Evidently, this summary was based on the original, authentic fax that Dallaire
sent to Gen. Baril at the DPKO in New York City, dated January 11, 1994.
But the summary of this document made no mention of an informant talking about an "anti-Tutsi extermination" plan or any of the other assertions
that appear in paragraphs 6 and 7 of the "Genocide Fax."

Seven days after the Khan review, on November 27, 1995, another fax
arrived at the DPKO in New York City, also bearing the subject heading
"Request for Protection for Informant." This fax reproduced a copy of
the two-page document that is now known as the "Genocide Fax," including paragraphs 6 and 7, and reporting about an informant who talked
about "anti-Tutsi extermination" (etc.).

But the fax that arrived at the DPKO on November 27 also contained
other peculiar features that are missing from the copy of the "Genocide
Fax" that Dobbs has posted online. At the top left-hand corner of the November 27 fax, a UN employee named Lamin J. Sise has typed: "This
cable was not found in DPKO files. The present copy was placed in the
files on 28 November 1995. Lamin J. Sise. 28 Nov. 1995." Additionally,
the sender's date-stamp that runs across the very top of both pages of the
fax reads: "From : Connaughton – Camberley, Surrey Phone No. : 01276
25210 Nov. 27, 1995 8:11PM F04."

Richard M. Connaughton was then a colonel in the British military and
is a historian of military affairs. "Camberley, Surrey" suggests a connection with the British Royal Military Academy at Sandhurst in southern
England, where the British Army trains its officers. So the copy of the
"Genocide Fax" as it exists today actually dates from November 27, 1995,
not January 11, 1994. Moreover, it came from (presumably) a colonel
serving at the RMAS.

As Christopher Black, a Canadian defense attorney and the attorney
for Gen. Augustin Ndindiliyimana in the Military II trial before the ICTR,
explains these peculiarities:

> [T]he copy of this document presented by the Prosecutor at the
> ICTR…has had the name and fax number of the sender, Sise's

note and other notes removed. It is this doctored version of the cable that the Prosecutor tried to present as an exhibit in the Military II in October, 2005.... General Dallaire does not mention such a fax before November 1995.... There was no response from New York to such a fax. There exist only responses to a fax concerning weapons caches, but this original fax is nowhere to be found. It is clear that Dallaire sent a fax that night [January 11, 1994] and that it concerned only weapons caches and seeking advice from New York regarding the protection of the informant. In fact, the subject heading of the "genocide" fax is not "genocide" or "killing" but an innocuous "Request For Protection of Informant." The present fax was fabricated using the original fax which dealt with weapons caches only by cutting out some of the paragraphs of that fax and pasting in new paragraphs about killing Tutsis and Belgians.[198]

We concur. Apparently, the original fax sent by Dallaire on January 11, 1994 to the DPKO in New York City made no mention of an "anti-Tutsi extermination" plan. But this fax has "disappeared"—expunged from the DPKO's archive. Then from November 27-28, 1995 onward, the counterfeit so-called "Genocide Fax" was put in its place. The significance of the "Genocide Fax," of course, is that it can be used as a documentary record of early UN knowledge of Hutu planning to "exterminate" Tutsi. The counterfeit fax thus reinforces the common and indeed regnant belief about a Hutu "conspiracy" to commit genocide, just as it reinforces the regnant belief about the UN's "failure" to act on this knowledge.

There is other evidence that the fax introduced on November 27-28, 1995 is a doctored version of the original. One is that Dallaire's superior at UNAMIR at the time, the Secretary-General's Special Representative Jacques-Roger Booh-Booh, categorically denies that he ever read a fax that mentioned anything other than an informant who warned of Hutu weapons caches, or that he and Dallaire ever discussed anything other than these weapons caches.[199] Another is that if Dallaire ever possessed credible evidence of genocidal intent against the Tutsi, he assuredly would have warned his own UNAMIR troops and the supposedly threatened

Belgians. But there is no record of his ever having done so.

We believe that it is important to recognize the extent to which Dallaire in his role as UNAMIR force commander served as a tool of Western powers supporting the RPF (the United States, Britain, and Canada), and is therefore unreliable not only with respect to the "Genocide Fax," but as regards Rwanda 1994 more generally. Dallaire was blatantly hostile to the French, opposing their attempt to establish and maintain a civilian refuge area during the mass killing (Operation Turquoise), rejecting their offer to look into the shoot-down as they had on-the-spot personnel in Kigali (Dallaire preferred to wait for the import of U.S. experts from Germany). While concerned with FAR weapons caches and threats he ignored the massive RPF buildup of arms and cadres that were quickly put into action on and after April 6. And he supported the reduction of UN forces in Rwanda, paralleling the U.S.-U.K.- Kagame position. He was an utter failure insofar as UNAMIR was supposedly in place to prevent war and mass slaughter.

Dallaire never publicized the existence of the fax until November 1995, at which time it was first reported in Belgian and British newspapers, and only *after* which time it conveniently showed up at the DPKO in New York City. Booh-Booh notes how "bizarre" he found it that even though UNAMIR received numerous reports that the RPF was receiving arms shipments from Uganda, Dallaire never acted on this information to interdict the shipments, but remained focused on FAR weapons caches instead.[200] Amadou Deme, a Senegalese officer who served in UNAMIR's intelligence section, recounted the many steps that UNAMIR knew the RPF had taken in "preparation for hostilities" leading up to April 6: The "build up [of] forces, logistics, stocks, etc.," the "bringing of troops, the information of massive weapons and ammunition from Uganda,…likely from the Ugandan [People's Defense Force]," the lack of access by "our observers in the RPF zone," and the like.[201] All of this reflects UNAMIR knowledge of the RPF's buildup towards its final offensive, not Hutu preparations for genocide. And we've already noted Dallaire's August 1993 assessment that "[the RPF] displayed the potential to easily defeat the [FAR]."

A remarkable feature of the importance given the "Genocide Fax" is its source, Jean-Pierre Turatsinze, a supposed informant on high-level

Hutu plans, who allegedly told UNAMIR Force Commander Dallaire that Hutu leaders intended to exterminate the Tutsi (to paraphrase the extant fax's "anti-Tutsi extermination" theme). Actually, the fax doesn't even state that Jean-Pierre *knew* of such a plan—merely that he was allegedly "ordered to register all Tutsi in Kagali" and that "He *suspects* it is for their extermination..." (emphasis added). So the plan is only a figment of Jean-Pierre's imagination, whether or not he really believed it.

But who was he? Alison Des Forges greatly exaggerated the significance of Jean-Pierre, claiming that he "reported directly to the chief of staff of the Rwandan army and to the president of the MRND,"[202] but she gives no evidence for this. For Faustin Twagirimungu, at the time the prime minister-designate and the head of the *Mouvement Démocratrique Républicain*, one of the Hutu opposition parties, the man who called the existence of this informant to UNAMIR's attention, and who would become the first prime minister of the successor government after the RPF seized power later that year, Jean-Pierre was nothing more than an "office boy for MRND, but an office boy who was also kind of [an] insurgent guide for RPF. Because, finally, he left the country, and he joined RPF."[203] Amadou Deme, one of four UNAMIR officers to meet with Jean-Pierre on January 10 and thereafter (the others were the Belgian Col. Luc Marchal, the Belgian Col. Henry Kesteloot, and the Belgian Capt. Frank Claeys—Dallaire himself never met Jean-Pierre), writes that the only evidence of Hutu violations that Jean-Pierre ever produced were roughly three dozen AK-47s, ammunition clips, and grenades—and "that was all regarding the famous reconnaissance of the MRND weapons cache."[204]

So why would the Western establishment latch on to some words from a figure such as Jean-Pierre, uncorroborated by documentary or other evidence? And why have his vague claims, which did not even encompass claims of a known plan, have been taken seriously ever since? The contrast with the establishment's treatment of the findings of Michael Hourigan's National Team, of compelling witness evidence of grave wrongdoing by the RPF, buried by the ICTR's chief prosecutor, is dramatic, but fits well the fact that politics readily overrides truth in the propaganda system. Jean-Pierre's unverified claims fit Western propaganda needs; Hourigan's far more solid findings did not. Therefore, whereas Jean-Pierre and the "Genocide Fax" can resurface during the twentieth anniversary of the

"Rwandan genocide," Hourigan's National Team findings cannot. The only surprise is that in the trial at the ICTR known as Military I, when finding all four defendants not guilty of the "conspiracy to commit genocide" charge, the trial chamber also dismissed the evidence provided by "informant Jean-Pierre" due to "lingering questions concerning [his] reliability...."[205]

If all of this is true, we would suggest that Dallaire should be regarded as a war criminal for positively facilitating the actual mass killings of April-July, rather than taken as a hero for giving allegedly disregarded warnings that might have stopped them.

11. The *New York Times* and other "Genocide Fax" disinformants

As we have seen throughout, bodies of fact incompatible with the standard model—on the April 6, 1994 shoot-down/assassination, the RPF's responsibility for and readiness to move after the shoot-down, the relative numbers of Hutu and Tutsi dead, the active engagement of the United States and its closest allies in support of RPF objectives, the alleged Hutu "conspiracy to commit genocide"—are simply blacked out in the establishment media, and advocates for the accepted view can spew out falsehoods or play dumb without contestation.

Thus Michael Dobbs can play dumb on the shoot-down and active U.S. and allied participation in the ongoing Rwanda events, and continue the falsification of the "Genocide Fax" tale without correction (in his "Rwanda's Shrouded Nightmare"[206]). Although the *Times* did publish three letters in response to Dobbs's commentary,[207] none challenged the authenticity of the "Genocide Fax," and none challenged the standard model's Hutu "conspiracy to commit genocide." In fact, one letter signed by Linda Melvern, Larry Stanton, and co-signed by 9 other "academics, authors, and international lawyers," heaped falsehood upon falsehood, claiming that the discredited "informant," Jean-Pierre, was credible, that "there was ample evidence for a genocide conspiracy that did not rely on Jean-Pierre," and that Dobbs had failed to mention the "overwhelming evidence of planning that persuaded the judges of the tribunal to convict defendants of conspiracy to commit genocide."[208]

But as we pointed out in Section 7 above, and show again in Appendix I, of the 15 defendants in the four major trials at the ICTR, *all 15 were acquitted of the "conspiracy to commit genocide" charge*—indicating that even the NATO-power vetted ICTR's judges have not been persuaded to "convict defendants of conspiracy to commit genocide." Given this fact, it would have been more honest had the 11 co-signers written instead that the ICTR's stunning record of acquittals and reversals on appeal on the conspiracy charge has only been broken following some early machinations by the Prosecution to seek guilty plea agreements through malpractice and coercion, as in the case of Jean Kambanda. But now we are talking about the role of integrity in the prospering field of "Genocide Studies," one that is remarkably politicized.

Gerald Caplan was also among the 11 co-signers of the letter to the *New York Times*. In the Organization of African Unity's 2000 report *Rwanda: The Preventable Genocide*, Caplan *et al.* addressed the "Genocide Fax." Echoing both Philip Gourevitch's (1998) and Human Rights Watch's (1999) earlier conflation of the Connaughton version of the fax with the now missing original version of it, the OAU report treats Jean-Pierre as a credible source as well as repeating the "anti-Tutsi extermination" theme. Although this report accurately summarizes the response that the Department of Peacekeeping Operations in New York City sent back to Dallaire, "denying him permission to seize the arms caches revealed by Jean-Pierre," it fails to notice the discrepancy between the DPKO's response about arms caches and the alleged extermination theme of the fax.[209] Well before 2000, the apocryphal "Genocide Fax" had successfully supplanted the original within the establishment histories of Rwanda 1994.

In a personal attack on Michael Dobbs that Caplan posted to the *Rabble.ca* website, Caplan took issue with the "central proposition" of Dobb's *New York Times* commentary: "Whether," in Dobbs's words, "the genocide was planned, and was thus foreseeable, has been hotly debated by scholars, politicians and lawyers."[210] Caplan also let it slip that he and the other co-signers had sent "another letter in confidence to the head of the [Holocaust Memorial] Museum," and that "several members of our group contacted senior Museum officials. We demanded the obvious:

that Dobbs' piece be immediately removed from the Museum website."[211]

Aside from the fact that Caplan and his associates here show themselves to be "Rwandan genocide-" enforcers ready to engage in academic repression whenever someone challenges the standard model, Caplan is onto something important. As regards Dobbs, Caplan writes that "If [the genocide] were unplanned, that meant the killings were spontaneous. If so, perhaps there was no intent to exterminate all Tutsi. If so, according to the 1948 UN Convention on the Prevention and Punishment of the Crime of Genocide, there was no genocide at all."

This logical—indeed dangerous—conclusion is what so infuriated Caplan *et al.*, and mobilized them to attack Dobbs at both the *New York Times* and Holocaust Memorial Museum. If no plan existed among Rwanda's Hutu population prior to the assassination of Habyarimana to exterminate the country's Tutsi population, then, as Caplan concedes, the Hutu-side of the killings that began late that night and the next day must have been "spontaneous," a response to the crisis that engulfed the country.[212] For Caplan, however, this conclusion is unacceptable. Either there was a Hutu plan to exterminate the Tutsi, or "there was no genocide at all." But this *either-or* is both historically false as well as illogical; an alternative explanation comes to mind (ours), but they cannot conceive of the possibility that the mass killings of 1994 stemmed mainly from RPF plans and actions. Nor can they allow this thought to have a public hearing. And if and when it does, they must attack and slander whoever gives it a hearing; as we have seen, such people are guilty of "genocide denial," "revisionism," and the like.[213] Surely, Kagame-Power's attack and slander apparatus is grateful for all of the assistance they provide it.[214]

Both Christopher Black and one of the present authors (Peterson) also submitted letters to the editor of the *New York Times* challenging Dobbs's treatment of the "Genocide Fax," though of course from different angles than did Melvern and associates. Black engaged in a number of email exchanges with *Times* editors as well as with Dobbs himself in an effort to show them the error of their ways, and Peterson engaged with *Times* editors over the co-signed letter's patent falsehoods. But neither Black nor Peterson were able to persuade the *Times* to publish any version of their rebuttals. Today, the truth of the Hutu-based "Rwandan genocide" remains so deeply ingrained in the collective mindset of much of the

world that obvious facts cannot penetrate, and falsehoods are institutionalized and defended by power and by the emotional attachments to the
party-line.

12. Role of UN, human rights groups, media, and intellectuals in promulgating the standard model

As an organization, the United Nations is heavily dependent on the
policies and actions of its Member States. Generally speaking, the more
powerful a Member State outside the UN, the more powerful it will be in
the UN, particularly in its relations to the Security Council and the Exec-
utive Office of the Secretary-General. On many issues, the UN can be
managed by determined Great Powers.

The United States and its close allies, the U.K. and Canada, have
guided the UN on Rwanda-related issues since the early 1990s. They
arranged for the establishment of the ICTR and greatly influenced its
work, their muscle appearing most dramatically in their ability to quash
the Hourigan investigation and otherwise prevent the ICTR from investigating the assassination of Habyarimana; in their ability to get the Gersony report that featured RPF civilian massacres kept out of public
view;[215] and in their ability to use the ICTR to prosecute their Hutu enemies from 1994, and to sustain the culture of RPF impunity through the
present day.

In a stunning event, they were also able to get the Security Council to
make official the standard model's foundational lie that there was a "1994
Genocide against the Tutsi in Rwanda," to quote from Resolution 2150,[216]
which the Council adopted on April 16, 2014, during a session devoted
to the "Prevention and fight against genocide."[217] That day, ambassadors
mentioned Rwanda 140 times during the session, a staggering total. Resolution 2150 recalls the decision by the ICTR appeals chamber in June
2006 that "it was a 'fact of common knowledge' that 'between 6 April
and 17 July 1994, there was a genocide in Rwanda against the Tutsi ethnic
group'," and that the appeals chamber had taken "judicial notice" of this.
Moreover, the Resolution "*Condemns without reservation* any denial of
this Genocide, and *urges* Member states to develop educational programs

that will inculcate future generations with the lessons of the Genocide in order to prevent future genocides...."[218] This was a "landmark decision," the U.S. Holocaust Memorial Museum reported.[219] We do not believe that the Security Council has ever been used in this manner previously (i.e., to issue a proclamation about the truth of an historical event), not even as regards the Nazi-managed holocaust. In 2014, Kagame Power had reached its pinnacle.

Human rights groups played an ugly role in the mass killings in Rwanda. Major organizations like Human Rights Watch and Amnesty International as a matter of policy ignore the crime of aggression and focus on war crimes carried out in the wake of aggressions, as they did in the cases of the U.S. attacks on the Federal Republic of Yugoslavia and Iraq. This is very convenient for the United States, given its prolific record of aggression in recent decades.[220] In the case of Rwanda, this exclusion allowed human rights groups to ignore the RPF's aggression from Uganda in 1990 and later, and to ignore the RPF's illegal occupation of parts of three prefectures in the north, while focusing on the Habyarimana government's responsive crackdown on the invaders and their suspected local allies.

We noted in Section 2 that as early as March 1993, the International Commission of Inquiry into Human Rights Abuses in Rwanda had begun to frame Habyarimana and his close associates with accusations of "genocide."[221] Some months later, in August 1993, the UN's first Special Rapporteur on Rwanda concluded that certain massacres and acts of intercommunal violence "could fall within" the Genocide Convention.[222] Thus as early as 1993, these two baseless and politicized findings for Rwanda served to establish the dominant interpretive framework for much of the reporting on Rwanda that followed. Neither of these reports had much to say about the RPF invasion and ethnic cleansing which pushed out and turned into refugees several hundred thousand Hutu farmers. Alison Des Forges, a co-chair of the International Commission, claimed later that its report "put Rwanda human rights abuses squarely before the international community."[223] The RPF used this report as justification for a new killing spree. We believe that this and other reports and claims of supposed human rights groups contributed substantially to the demonization of the Habyarimana government and Rwanda's Hutu population more generally, to wide support for the RPF, and thus to the serial genocides carried out by the RPF in Rwanda and then Zaire-DRC.

Alison Des Forges was an important figure both in tearing down the Habyarimana and subsequent interim government and in building support for the RPF, with a stream of human rights documents, articles, public advocacy, and eventual witness-for-the-prosecution testimony at the ICTR, all based on the standard model and delivered by her as an expert on Rwanda and a human rights advocate. In global media citations in relation to Rwanda after October 1, 1990, Des Forges received 939 mentions, even though she has been dead since February 12, 2009.[224] Des Forges also played a more direct political role, with her Human Rights Watch colleagues lobbying at the United Nations in New York City in May 1994 to get the relevant delegations to recognize RPF representatives and to discredit those of the Rwandan interim government.[225] Less well known and less publicized was the fact that she had been a consultant with the U.S. State Department in the early 1990s, and for many years had engaged in what her own *Curriculum Vitae* described as "advocacy and information meetings" with the Pentagon and U.S. National Security Council, members of Congress, delegations to the United Nations (the United States, France, Belgium, and Britain are named), members of the UN Secretariat, and the editorial boards of the *New York Times* and *Washington Post*, among other venues.[226] This is of course unmentioned by the establishment media, and probably would not influence views of her independence and objectivity.

In "Propaganda and Practice," one section of her *"Leave None To Tell the Story"*, Des Forges manages to take what has now been the RPF's actual practices for the past 24 years and attribute 100 percent of them to "Hutu Power."[227] In this upside-down section, she writes about a "mimeographed document entitled *'Note Relative à la Propagande d'-Expansion et de Recrutement'*," allegedly discovered by accident somewhere in Butare prefecture, sometime after the RPF's victory. In this document, "one propagandist tells others how to sway the public most effectively," she writes. For "propagandist," read *Hutu* propagandist. Indeed, Des Forges uses the word "propagandist(s)" 49 times in the section alone, and "propaganda" another 12 times, always in reference to Hutu propagandists.

Des Forges's Hutu propagandist draws ideas and inspiration from Roger Mucchielli's 1970 book, *Psychologie de la publicité et de la propaganda*, as well as Lenin and Goebbels. This Hutu propagandist "proposes two techniques that were to become often used in Rwanda" by the Hutu. "The first is to 'create' events to lend credence to propaganda." Her example was the RPF's " 'attack' on Kigali on October 4-5, 1990"— an attack that actually did occur, based on clandestine RPF cells already present in Kigali.[228]

Her Hutu propagandist "calls his second proposal 'Accusation in a mirror', meaning his colleagues should impute to his enemies exactly what they and their own party are planning to do." Unable to detect the irony in attributing ideas such as these to a Hutu propagandist, Des Forges adds that "with such a tactic, propagandists can persuade listeners and 'honest people' that they are being attacked and are justified in taking whatever measures are necessary 'for legitimate [self-] defense'."[229] As we've seen throughout, these passages are perfectly accurate descriptions not only of the RPF's propaganda (e.g., its repeated warnings of a planned Hutu genocide against the Tutsi to justify its war on the Habyarimana government and, later, against Zaire-DRC as well)—but also of Alison Des Forges's. In a subsection titled "*Restoring the Old Regime*," Des Forges writes: "From the first days of the war, officials and [Hutu] propagandists alike warned that the RPF had come to re-establish their total Tutsi control over the Hutu."[230] But Des Forges treats this as nothing more than Hutu propaganda, even though total RPF control over Rwanda's Hutu population has been a fact on the ground for most of the past 20 years!

Conflicts of interest among the standard model experts are commonplace. One of the most influential commentators on Rwanda has been Philip Gourevitch, a feature writer for *The New Yorker*, whose 1998 book *We wish to inform you that tomorrow we will be killed with our families: Stories from Rwanda* was a rare popular essay on Rwanda 1994. Along with Des Forges, Gourevitch has been perhaps the best-known U.S. commentator on the subject. He was an important disseminator of the "Genocide Fax,"[231] the authenticity of which he has never questioned. Not well known was the fact that he was in the late 1990s the brother-in-law of James Rubin, the Assistant Secretary of State for Public Affairs in the Clinton administration,[232] and likely source of the "Genocide Fax."

Gourevitch's main conflict of interest, though, is with himself: An ardent admirer of Paul Kagame and an advocate for Kagame Power, everything he writes reflects these facts. For Gourevitch, Rwanda 1994 *is* a story of good guys and bad guys.[233] He likes to quote Kagame lavishly and uncritically, as when Kagame told him, "Personally, I have no problem with telling the truth;" Gourevitch used this insight into the great man's soul to conclude that "In a world where politicians were presumed to be liars, Kagame had found that one could often gain a surprise advantage by not being false."[234]

Gourevitch has also been a vulgar apologist for RPF attacks on Hutu refugees in Rwanda and later Zaire-DRC. He makes the RPF's April 1995 massacre of at least 4,000 internally displaced Hutu at the Kibeho camp in southern Rwanda into a kind of national purification following the "genocide"—after all, there were "*génocidaires*" at Kibeho.[235] He even accepts the far-fetched results of the so-called Independent International Commission of Inquiry into the events at Kibeho ("The tragedy of Kibeho neither resulted from a planned action by Rwandan authorities to kill a certain group of people, nor was it an accident that could have been prevented."[236]) as genuine and fair—exactly as the RPF did.[237] As for the much larger Hutu refugee camps in Zaire-DRC, Gourevitch descends to the outrageous. Many of the refugees did not deserve refugee status— they were "fugitives fleeing criminal prosecution" in Kagame's newly liberated Rwanda, and "all of us who paid taxes in countries that paid the UNHCR...were feeding [them]." Worse, he complains that "breeding more Hutus was Hutu Power policy" at these camps, so we were paying for that, too. The "Hutu Power patronage network" really had it nice in the camps. Free food, water, sanitation, medical care, well-stocked pharmacies, two-story video bars, libraries, churches, brothels, photo studios—the camps were a veritable land of "refugee entitlements" and "rump genocidal state" all in one.[238] This is possibly the sickest performance of the many apologists for a real genocide.

Looking at media bias on Rwanda more broadly, Table 2 represents relative access to the world's media according to two broad categories: Does the potential contributor toe the party-line on the "Rwandan genocide" (as exemplified by figures such as Paul Kagame, his foreign minister Louise Mushikiwabo, Roméo Dallaire, Gerald Caplan, and Linda

Melvern)? Or does the potential contributor dissent from one or more key components of the party-line (as exemplified by figures such as the former Kagame allies Faustin Twagiramungu and Theogene Rudasingwa, and by Robin Philpot, Christopher Black, Peter Erlinder, Christian Davenport, and Allan Stam)?

The first numbers that jump out at us are the totals: Over the ten year period through April 30, 2014, individuals with a history of advocacy for the standard model of the "Rwandan genocide" were published ten-and-one-half times as frequently as persons whose work dissents from the standard model (181 to 17). During this period, Paul Kagame's byline alone appeared as many times as the group of 20 dissenters (17).[239] Serious dissent from the standard model means exclusion from (and often ridicule by) virtually all media discussion that turns on the events in Rwanda 1994.

Table 2 appears on the following page.

Table 2. Bylined-articles on Rwanda in the world's media, April 1, 2004 - April 30, 2014[240]

20 Advocates for the Standard Model of the "Rwandan Genocide"		20 Dissenters from the Standard Model of the "Rwandan Genocide"	
Gerald Caplan:	30	Pierre Péan:	9
Linda Melvern:	27	Robin Philpot:	2
Roméo Dallaire:	25	Theogene Rudasingwa:	2
Paul Kagame:	17	Keith Harmon Snow:	2
Colette Braeckman:	13	Jacques-Roger Booh-Booh:	1
Louise Mushikiwabo:	12	Peter Erlinder:	1
Gary J. Bass:	8	Luc Marchal:	0
Mahmood Mamdani:	7	Christopher Black:	0
Samantha Power:	6	Barrie Collins:	0
Philip Gourevitch:	6	Thierry Cruvellier:	0
Fergal Keane:	6	Christian Davenport:	0
Ben Kiernan:	4	Amadou Deme:	0
Deborah Lipstadt:	4	Tiphaine Dickson:	0
Tony Blair:	3	Charles Kambanda:	0
Daniel Jonah Goldhagen:	3	Bernard Lugan:	0
Samuel Totten:	3	Charles Onana:	0
Michael Barnett:	2	Peter Robinson:	0
Bill Clinton:	2	Allan Stam:	0
Herman J. Cohen:	2	Helmut Strizek:	0
Rakiya Omaar:	1	Faustin Twagiramungu:	0
TOTAL	181	TOTAL	17

But beyond the number totals a further lesson lies in the media venues of standard model spokespersons and the dissenters. The fact that Kagame has been provided with space to "talk his book" twice in the *Wall Street Journal* (including one on April 7, 2014[241]) and twice in *The Times* of London we believe to be very significant, as is the fact that his colleague Louise Mushikiwabo has also enjoyed substantial access, including two commentaries in *The Independent* (London). This has been the pattern throughout. Advocates for the standard model enjoy not just access—they enjoy access to major media outlets. Whereas ardent Kagame-apologist Gerald Caplan's byline on Rwanda has dominated the establishment Canadian media and been a mainstay at the prestigious Toronto *Globe and Mail*, Linda Melvern's byline a mainstay at *The Guardian* (7 commentaries in all, while none of our 20 dissenters had any), and Roméo Dallaire appears to be able to publish on this topic anywhere he chooses around Canada as well as at the *New York Times*, our 20 dissenters (with the exception of the French writer Pierre Péan) have been limited to politically marginal media venues such as the online Global Research (3) and Dissident Voice (1) websites, the allAfrica aggregator website (2), the Montreal-based French-language newspaper, *Le Devoir* (1), and France's *Le Figaro* (1). However, the number of dissenters is inflated by the fact that one of them, Pierre Péan, published 9 of the 17 items, all in French publications, none of the first rank in circulation.[242] These results underscore the fact that like his cohorts, Péan, a distinguished French journalist, has had zero access to establishment English-language media venues, which systematically operate in a universe where the ultimate criterion for inclusion is service to power.

This modest list exhausts the dissenters' access. Over the ten-year period our survey covers, no less than 14 out of the 20 dissenters had zero byline access to express their perspectives. But this is clearly not because they have had nothing to say on the topic of the "Rwandan genocide." The party line makes them genocide deniers, hence properly ignored, although as we have contended here they are actually opposing the misallocation of responsibility for genocide (in Rwanda) and apologetics for a second and larger genocide (DRC).

Concluding Note: Genocidist misallocation (Rwanda) and the real genocide denial (DRC)

We have stressed that when examined closely, all of the major themes incorporated in the establishment story of the "Rwandan genocide" unravel before our eyes. "Rwandan Hutus in 1994 could freely, joyfully, and systematically slaughter 8,000 Tutsi a day for 100 days without any foreign interference," Samantha Power has written,[243] condensing three key misleading elements into a single sentence: That foreign powers stood idly by while massive killing took place, that 800,000 Tutsi were slaughtered, and that as an invading force from Uganda, the RPF doesn't count among the foreign powers, but must have been one of the indigenous forces engaged in a civil war.

We have seen that the notion of a Hutu "conspiracy to commit genocide"—the most fundamental claim of all—has completely unraveled, and in the most interesting of venues: The trial and appeals chambers of the ICTR itself. We have also seen that as of the second-half of 1993, the RPF had already achieved military superiority over the Armed Forces of Rwanda, and that this was the assessment of Dallaire's Reconnaissance Mission to Rwanda in August of that year, which he duly reported to the UN Secretary-General the following month. And we have seen how the RPF, having fought for power in Rwanda for three-and-a-half years, ultimately stood to lose their war under the Arusha Accords, as the national elections called for by them could only end in a landslide defeat for their ethnic Tutsi, who comprised some 10 percent of the population at most. The result: The RPF leadership's decision to assassinate Habyarimana, to launch the final offensive the very same evening, and to seize state power through extreme violence over the next 100 days.[244]

"More than 800,000 people were systematically killed—overwhelmingly the Tutsi, and also moderate Hutu, Twa and others," UN Secretary-General Ban Ki-moon said during the twentieth anniversary ceremony in Kigali.[245] We have shown that this, too, is a major lie, and that the evidence is clear that Hutu were the primary victims, which is entirely plausible given the RPF's military superiority and rapid victory. It also explains why the United States and its allies and the UN did not intervene to stop the bloodshed: They supported Paul Kagame at all times. And as he was on the road to victory and wanted no outside interference, the United States and the rest of the "international community" obliged him, viewing the huge bloodbath as acceptable "collateral damage," with hypocritical apologies to follow. But this policy went beyond non-intervention—Kagame was supported logistically and diplomatically, and the United States and its allies deliberately forced the reduction of UN troops as the mass killings escalated. Thus when Bill Clinton said in a 2013 interview that "If we'd gone in sooner, I believe we could have saved at least a third of the lives that were lost...it had an enduring impact on me,"[246] he managed to combine an implicit lie with rank hypocrisy.

We have also stressed that the U.S., U.K., and allied support of the Kagame-RPF invasion, subversion, mass killing and conquest of Rwanda was followed up within two years by the U.S.-U.K.-supported Kagame-Museveni invasion and mass killings in Zaire-DRC. Through the present day, this involved the eventual deaths of several million local civilians and Hutu refugees, greatly exceeding the numbers that perished in the "Rwandan genocide." Still ongoing, this was done under the guise of pursuing Hutu "*génocidaires*" in Zaire-DRC, a serviceable cover for the pursuit of material and geopolitical aims on the part of both the local killer-managers (Kagame *et al*) and their major supporters (the United States *et al*). The "*génocidaire*" excuse was swallowed in the West and contributed, along with the quiet support of Kagame and Museveni, to very modest publicity in the United States and the usual failure of the UN to take any action against the true mass killers.

This kind of purposeful inaction has also extended to the International Criminal Court. First, we should note that in contrast to the situation in Rwanda 1994 (or in the former Yugoslavia during the 1990s), no *ad hoc* tribunal has ever been created by the Security Council for the sole purpose of prosecuting persons responsible for genocide and other serious violations of international humanitarian law committed in the territory of Zaire-DRC from 1996 onward (to paraphrase Resolution 955, which created the International Criminal Tribunal for Rwanda). Although the killing fields of Zaire-DRC dwarf those of Rwanda and even more so the former Yugoslavia, no new *ad hoc* tribunal is likely to materialize, either. As long as Kagame and Museveni remain useful tools of U.S. power in central Africa, they will remain beyond prosecution.

Second, and equally revealing, since its inception in July 2002, the ICC has only managed to bring indictments against six individuals operating in the eastern DRC, either in the Ituri district of Orientale Province or in North and South Kivu provinces. But none of these figures was a "Big Fish," to recall the language favored by the ICTR's Prosecution; instead, all six were local or regional militia leaders, some with ties to the Hutu refugees, some not, but all involved in one form or another with local resource exploitation and its protection racket.[247]

Of course, the ICC has never brought or even threatened to bring an indictment against the Biggest Fish in the Great Lakes pond: Paul Kagame, a man who remains eminently indictable for the actions of his forces in the DRC during the now 12-year period over which the ICC's temporal jurisdiction extends. Here we have yet another confirmation of the real culture of RPF impunity. To recall ICTR Chief Prosecutor Hassan Jallow's words (applicable to the supposedly more independent ICC): The Statute of the ICC itself does not require the prosecution of *all* offenders—a maxim that we might inscribe on the tombstone of "international justice" as the Great Powers bury it in the first decades of the 21st century. As with common usage of the term "genocide," the bringing of indictments for the crime of genocide is always political, and follows a simple rule: Only the enemies of the Great White Northern Powers commit "genocide" for which they may be charged and prosecuted by a tribunal, whether *ad hoc* or permanent, but never these powers, and never their allies and clients.[248] In Mrs. Sheldon's famous response to the question, "Why should King Leopold be afraid of submitting his case to the Hague tribunal?" as recounted by the British journalist William Thomas Stead in 1905, she explained: "Men do not go to the gallows and put their heads in a noose if they can avoid it."[249] But this is precisely what the standard model of the "Rwandan genocide" has enabled for the past 20 years, as it has played its insidious Orwellian role, camouflaging the RPF's real genocides against millions of people first in Rwanda and then Zaire-DRC, while awarding these real *génocidaires* with a "victims'" license to go right on killing.[250]

"Historical clarity is a duty of memory that we cannot escape," Paul Kagame said at the twentieth anniversary ceremony in Kigali. "Behind the words 'Never Again', there is a story whose truth must be told in full, no matter how uncomfortable."[251]

At this stage it should be unnecessary to note that these words were spoken by a man who is quite possibly the greatest mass murderer alive today. However, the fact that Paul Kagame—as King Leopold II of Belgium once did (1865-1909)—continues to live and work freely in the world, unthreatened by "international justice," celebrated as the Abe Lincoln of his war-torn domain in central Africa, and highly regarded and honored in the United States, Britain, and Canada, shows us unambiguously that when the events in Rwanda 1994 are the issue, things as fragile as truth and historical clarity are only able to survive as exiles from these powers. From today on, it is time to start calling the exiles home.

Appendix I: More on the alleged Hutu "conspiracy to commit genocide" that never was

As noted in Section 7, the ICTR's trial and appeals chambers have been doing something that we find quite remarkable, given the ICTR's overall pro-RPF and anti-Hutu political role and biases: In their judgments, they have been either acquitting Hutu defendants on the "conspiracy to commit genocide" charge, or reversing on appeal previous convictions on this charge.

Here we'd like to briefly summarize the judgments in the major cases as regards the "conspiracy to commit genocide" charge, reiterating what we stated in Section 7: That a Hutu "conspiracy to commit genocide" refers to a conspiracy that existed some time *prior* to April 6, 1994, so that once the assassination of Habyarimana had been carried out, the Hutu conspirators could also carry out their *plan* to exterminate the Tutsi.

In the Government I trial of Édouard Karemera, a leading figure in the *Mouvement Républicain National pour la Démocratie et le Développement*, and who later served as the Minister of the Interior for the interim government, and Matthieu Ngirumpatse, president of the MRND, the oral summary of the verdict read out in court in December 2011 was stunning. "The Prosecution has not proved beyond a reasonable doubt that Karemera and Ngirumpatse, or other leaders, planned the massacre of Tutsis in advance of the assassination of President Habyarimana," Judge Dennis Byron said. "The Chamber acknowledges that the genocide may have started as a spontaneous reaction to the assassination of President Habyarimana, which was fuelled by the belief that the Tutsi-led RPF was responsible, and prior anti-Tutsi propaganda."[252]

Comparable acquittals or reversals on appeal were also handed down in the other 12 major cases known as Government II, Military I, and Military II. Taking them in the order in which the relevant judgments were delivered, with the four acquittals on the conspiracy charge in the Military I trial preceding the rest (including the aforementioned Government I acquittals), and doubtless establishing a precedent on this charge for all of the judgments that followed:

Military I Trial

Théoneste Bagosora : "NOT GUILTY of Conspiracy to Commit Genocide." (Judge Erik Møse *et al.*, *Judgment, Prosecutor v. Théoneste Bagosora et al.*, Case No. ICTR-98-41-T, December 18, 2008, para. 2258, p. 568, < http://tinyurl.com/ncarqtd >.)

Gratien Kabiligi : "NOT GUILTY of Conspiracy to Commit Genocide." (*Ibid.*, para. 2258, p. 568, < http://tinyurl.com/ncarqtd >.)

Aloys Ntabakuze : "NOT GUILTY of Conspiracy to Commit Genocide." (*Ibid.*, para. 2258, p. 569, < http://tinyurl.com/ncarqtd >.)

Anatole Nsengiyumva : "NOT GUILTY of Conspiracy to Commit Genocide." (*Ibid.*, para. 2258, p. 569, < http://tinyurl.com/ncarqtd >.)

Military II Trial

Augustin Ndindiliyimana : "Not Guilty of Conspiracy to Commit Genocide." (Judge Asoka de Silva *et al.*, *Judgment, Prosecutor v. Augustin Ndindiliyimana et al.*, Case No. ICTR-00-56-T, May 17, 2011, para. 262, p. 486, < http://tinyurl.com/mh3vzop >.)

Augustin Bizimungu : "Not Guilty of Conspiracy to Commit Genocide." (*Ibid.*, para. 262, p. 486, < http://tinyurl.com/mh3vzop >.)

François-Xavier Nzuwonemeye : "Not Guilty of Conspiracy to Commit Genocide." (*Ibid.*, para. 262, p. 486, < http://tinyurl.com/mh3vzop >.)

Innocent Sagahutu : "Not Guilty of Conspiracy to Commit Genocide." (*Ibid.*, para. 262, p. 487, < http://tinyurl.com/mh3vzop >.)

Government II Trial

Casimir Bizimungu : "NOT GUILTY of Conspiracy to Commit Genocide." (Judge Khalida Rachid Khan *et al.*, *Judgment, Prosecutor v. Casimir Bizimungu et al.*, Case No. ICTR-99-50-T, September 30, 2011, para. 1988, p. 538, < http://tinyurl.com/mc985pr >.)

Jérôme-Clément Bicamumpaka : "NOT GUILTY of Conspiracy to Commit Genocide." *(Ibid.*, para. 1988, p. 539, < http://tinyurl.com/mc985pr >.)

Justin Mugenzi : "The Appeals Chamber reverses, Judge Liu dissenting, Mugenzi's and Mugiraneza's convictions for conspiracy to commit genocide and enters a verdict of acquittal under Count 1 of the Indictment." (Judge Theodor Meron *et al.*, *Judgment on Appeal, Justin Mugenzi and Prosper Mugiraneza v. The Prosecutor*, Case No. ICTR-99-50-A, February 4, 2014, para. 94, p. 34, < http://tinyurl.com/mljl4un >.)

Prosper Mugiraneza : "The Appeals Chamber reverses, Judge Liu dissenting, Mugenzi's and Mugiraneza's convictions for conspiracy to commit genocide and enters a verdict of acquittal under Count 1 of the Indictment." *(Ibid.*, para. 94, p. 34, < http://tinyurl.com/mljl4un >.)

We also reviewed some of the other high-profile cases: Those of the three defendants in the "Role of the Media" trial, and the six defendants in the "Butare" trial. In eight out of nine of these cases, we found the same results: Straightforward acquittals or reversals on appeal.

Thus in the "Role of the Media" cases, allegedly based on broadcasts by *Radio Télévision Libre des Mille Collines* (RTLM) in association with its founder and Steering Committee member, Ferdinand Nahimana, and fellow Steering Committee member Jean-Bosco Barayagwiza, along with material published by *Kangura* magazine's Editor-in-Chief, Hassan Nzeze, the convictions of all three on the conspiracy charge were reversed on appeal. "The Appeals Chamber finds that a reasonable trier of fact could not conclude beyond reasonable doubt…that the only reasonable possible inference was that the Appellants had personally collaborated and organized institutional coordination between RTLM, the CDR[253] and *Kangura* with the specific purpose of committing genocide."[254]

Turning to the "Butare" cases: The Butare prefecture was the scene of massive amounts of violence in 1994 (including RPF killings of Hutu, as Robert Gersony's mission to Rwanda found[255]), and the six Hutu defendants were all accused of organizing the violence against Tutsi locally. Nevertheless, the trial chamber found five of these defendants "NOT GUILTY of Conspiracy to Commit Genocide"—only Pauline Nyiramasuhuko, the Minister for Family Welfare and Advancement of Women, was found "GUILTY of Conspiracy to Commit Genocide." [256] But even this verdict is self-contradictory, as none of Nyiramasuhuko's co-defendants (alleged co-conspirators) was found guilty on the conspiracy charge. Are we to believe that Nyiramasuhuko conspired with her co-conspirators, but her co-conspirators never conspired with her? Moreover, her alleged conspiracy began *on or after April 9, 1994,* so that by its timing alone, it falls outside what is understood as the Hutu "conspiracy to commit genocide." Nyiramasuhuko has appealed her conviction on the conspiracy charge, and we fully expect it to be reversed, like the others.

In the "Conspiracy to Commit Genocide" section in the *Judgment* rendered in the Military I trial—Col. Bagosora among the four defendants, a man often represented as the epitome of "Hutu Power" and the "mastermind of the genocide"—the trial chamber determined that:

> [I]n the context of the ongoing war with the RPF, [the] evidence does not invariably show that the purpose of arming and training these civilians or the preparation of lists was to kill Tutsi civilians. After the death of President Habyarimana, these tools were clearly put to use to facilitate killings. When viewed against the backdrop of the targeted killings and massive slaughter perpetrated by civilian and military assailants between April and July 1994 as well as earlier cycles of violence, it is understandable why for many this evidence takes on new meaning and shows a prior conspiracy to commit genocide. Indeed, these preparations are completely consistent with a plan to commit genocide. However, they are also consistent with preparations for a political or

military power struggle…. Accordingly, the Chamber is not sat-
isfied that the Prosecution has proven beyond reasonable doubt
that the four Accused conspired amongst themselves or with others to commit genocide before it unfolded on 7 April 1994.[257]

Adopting the logic of the Military I trial chamber—based in no small
part on the logic of the argument laid out in the May 2007 final trial brief
filed by the U.S. defense attorney Peter Erlinder on behalf of his client,
the former Para-Commando Battalion Commander, Major Aloys
Ntabakuze[258]—one could just as plausibly argue that when viewed against
the backdrop of its 46 month assault on the Rwandan government and
people, it is understandable why for critics of the standard model, the evidence of RPF killings and displacements leads to wholly different conclusions. For what it strongly suggests is that from some date prior to
October 1, 1990, until July 1994, the RPF's military and political leadership had conspired among themselves and with others to wage an aggressive war and to seize state power in Rwanda, with whatever suffering the
Tutsi might endure written-off as "collateral damage"—as "part of the
sacrifice," in Kagame's own words.[259] Indeed, according to Military I
logic, the RPF's execution of its 46 month war was completely consistent
with a plan to commit genocide against the Hutu, and to ethnically cleanse
Rwandan national territory of its Hutu and Tutsi collaborators.

Appendix II: The apocryphal "Genocide Fax"— another look

Copy A

```
                                          23 25 Z
                                             BP      TST

                       CNR 12                    10016678

                 OUTGOING CODE CABLE

DATE: 11 JANUARY 1994        HIR 57

TO: BARIL\DPKO\UNATIONS          FROM: DALLAIRE\UNAMIR\KIGALI
    NEW YORK

FAX NO:MOST IMMEDIATE-CODE        FAX NO: 011-250-84273
CABLE-212-963-9852
INMARSAT:

SUBJECT:REQUEST FOR PROTECTION FOR INFORMANT

ATTN: NGEN BARIL                  ROOM NO.2052

TOTAL NUMBER OF TRANSMITTED PAGES INCLUDING THIS ONE: 2

1.    FORCE COMMANDER PUT IN CONTACT WITH INFORMANT BY VERY VERY
IMPORTANT GOVERNMENT POLITICIAN.  INFORMANT IS A TOP LEVEL
TRAINER IN THE CADRE OF INTERHAMWE-ARMED MILITIA OF MRND.
```

Copy B

P 67   1/2
23 25 z
BP   TGT

CASE NO: ICTR-00-56-T
EXHIBIT NO: P.67
DATE ADMITTED. 11-10-2005
TENDERED BY: PROSECUTOR
NAME OF WITNESS FRANK CHESS   CNR 12   L0016678

OUTGOING CODE CABLE

DATE: 11 JANUARY 1994   HIR 67

TO: BARIL\DPKO\UNATIONS NEW YORK	FROM: DALLAIRE\UNAMIR\KIGALI
FAX NO:MOST IMMEDIATE-CODE CABLE-212-963-9852 INMARSAT:	FAX NO: 011-250-84273
SUBJECT:REQUEST FOR PROTECTION FOR INFORMANT	
ATTN: MGEN BARIL	ROOM NO.2052
TOTAL NUMBER OF TRANSMITTED PAGES INCLUDING THIS ONE: 2	

1. FORCE COMMANDER PUT IN CONTACT WITH INFORMANT BY VERY VERY IMPORTANT GOVERNMENT POLITICIAN. INFORMANT IS A TOP LEVEL TRAINER IN THE CADRE OF INTERHAMWE-ARMED MILITIA OF MRND.

Copy C

```
From : CONNAUGHTON   CAMBERLEY, SURREY   PHONE No : 01276 25210   NOV 27, 1995   8:11 PM   F04


This cable was not found      CASE NO....[CTR-00-56-T]........(mmm)  94/422 1/2
in DPKO files.  The present   EXHIBIT NO:...D.67.L...........  2315½
copy was placed in the        DATE ADMITTED....11-10-2005.........    TST
files on 28 November 1995.    ...ERED BY:....FRANK CARIS...
    ←─ J. S─e                 NAME OF WITNESS.....................
    LAMIN J. SISE                                    CWR/ 12
    28 Nov. 1995                                                      RECD
                                   OUTGOING CODE CABLE                   JAN 11 1994

       DATE: 11 JANUARY 1994          HIR 17

    ┌─────────────────────────────────────┬──────────────────────────────┐
    │ TO: BARIL\DPKO\UNATIONS             │ FROM: DALLAIRE\UNAMIR\KIGALI  │
    │     NEW YORK                        │                               │
    ├─────────────────────────────────────┼──────────────────────────────┤
    │ FAX NO:MOST IMMEDIATE-CODE          │ FAX NO: 011-350-84273         │
    │ CABLE-212-963-9852                  │                               │
    │ INMARSAT:                           │                               │
    ├─────────────────────────────────────┴──────────────────────────────┤
    │ SUBJECT:REQUEST FOR PROTECTION FOR INFORMANT                        │
    ├─────────────────────────────────────┬──────────────────────────────┤
    │ ATTN: MGEN BARIL                    │ ROOM NO.3052                  │
    ├─────────────────────────────────────┴──────────────────────────────┤
    │ TOTAL NUMBER OF TRANSMITTED PAGES INCLUDING THIS ONE:  2            │
    └─────────────────────────────────────────────────────────────────────┘

    1.   FORCE COMMANDER PUT IN CONTACT WITH INFORMANT BY VERY VERY
    IMPORTANT GOVERNMENT POLITICIAN.  INFORMANT IS A TOP LEVEL
    TRAINER IN THE CADRE OF INTERHAMWE-ARMED MILITIA OF MRND.
```

On this and the preceding two pages, we've reproduced the topmost sections of the first page of three different copies of the so-called "Genocide Fax"—the name that *The New Yorker*'s Philip Gourevitch gave in 1998[260] to the copy he possessed of an outgoing code cable from UNAMIR Force Commander Roméo Dallaire in Kigali, to the Canadian General Maurice Baril at the UN's Department of Peace-Keeping Operations in New York City, dated January 11, 1994.

As can be plainly seen in the address box of each of the three copies, the "Subject" that Dallaire *et al.* chose for this cable was "Request For Protection For Informant." This informant (though *disinformant* would more accurately describe him) was Jean-Pierre Turatsinze, a man who would shortly thereafter join the Rwandan Patriotic Front, if he wasn't already covertly working for the RPF.[261]

We will not deal with the contents of the "Genocide Fax" here; we've already dealt with its contents in Section 10 (above). In all three copies, however, the contents of the message are identical, word-for-word. Each copy has 12 numbered paragraphs; each copy skips paragraph 12 (i.e., contains paragraphs numbered 1 through 11 and 13, but not one numbered 12); and each copy is two pages in length.

But we do want to use the information provided by the three different copies of the "Genocide Fax"—particularly Copy C—to challenge its authenticity.

Copy A is the copy that Philip Gourevitch first wrote about in 1998, and it is the copy that Michael Dobbs reproduced in a commentary he published jointly at the websites of the United States Holocaust Memorial Museum and the National Security Archive in January 2014.[262] Notice that above the phrase "OUTGOING CODE CABLE" in Copy A, minimal information is provided.

Copy B is the copy that the Prosecution at the International Criminal Tribunal for Rwanda entered as exhibits during multiple trials of Hutu defendants. On this copy (B, but not Copy A), above and to the left of "OUTGOING CODE CABLE," is written that the Prosecutor in the trial of the Hutu former general in charge of Rwanda's Gendarmerie, Augustin Ndindiliyimana (Case No. ICTR-00-56-T), entered this document as an exhibit during the testimony of the Belgian Captain and former UNAMIR member Frank Claeys on October 11, 2005. But beyond the little bit of handwriting in the upper right-hand corner of this document, we find no other new information.

Not so with Copy C, which provides us with three clusters of new information that are absent from the other two copies.

First, unlike Copy A and Copy B, we see that on October 11, 2005, Copy C was entered as an exhibit in the trial of Augustin Ndindiliyimana, not by the Prosecutor, but by the general's defense attorney, the Canadian Christopher Black. (Of course, Black's name does not appear. But we know that Black served as the lead counsel in Ndindiliyimana's defense.) This fact is significant, as we will explain below.

Second, as we discussed in Section 10, we can see from the date-stamp that runs across the top of Copy C that it originated as a fax sent out on November 27, 1995 by "Connaughton" (i.e., Richard M. Connaughton, who was at that time a colonel in the British military and is today a historian of military affairs). The phrase "Camberley, Surrey" suggests that Connaughton has a connection with the British Royal Military Academy at Sandhurst in southern England, where the British Army trains its officers.[263]

Third, as we also discussed in Section 10, in the upper left-hand corner of Copy C, we read that "This cable was not found in DPKO files"—files that the UN's Department of Peace-Keeping Operations had searched in the weeks before. In early November 1995, Shaharyar Khan, the Secretary-General's Special Representative for Rwanda since July 1994, had ordered a review of the UN's files on Rwanda for the period October 1993 through March 1994. The Khan review of the UN files "confirm[ed] the view that there was no information or indication of planned genocide. There were, of course, warnings of armed clashes, violence and killings on an ethnic basis."[264] Thus, two-and-a-half years before Gourevitch published on the "Genocide Fax" in *The New Yorker*, the Khan review had found no record of any such document in the DPKO's Rwanda files. The information in the upper left-hand corner continues: "The present copy was placed in the files on 28 November 1995," and this fact is signed and attested to by Lamin J. Sise at the United Nations' headquarters in New York City.

So we learn from these three clusters of new information that there are serious problems with the authenticity of the "Genocide Fax." Since the oldest extant copy of a code cable dated January 11, 1994 from Dallaire in Kigali to Baril at the DPKO in New York City could not be found in the DPKO's Rwanda files when they were searched in early November 1995, and since it turns out that the oldest extant copy was only placed in the DPKO's files on November 28, 1995, after having been faxed to the DPKO by Colonel Richard Connaughton the prior day from the town of Camberley in the English county of Surrey, something is rotten with the "Genocide Fax."

Moreover, an important question demands to be answered: Since the oldest extant copy of this document (Copy C) includes the three clusters of information we've just reviewed (i.e., that Connaughton faxed it to the DPKO on November 27, 1995, that Sise placed it in the DPKO's Rwanda files on November 28, 1995, and that this vital information is missing from the other two copies of the fax), why do both the Gourevitch-Dobbs copy of the document (Copy A) and the ICTR-Prosecution copy of the document (Copy B) leave out this vital information?

Christopher Black, the attorney who represented General Ndindiliyimana at his trial before the ICTR, wrote to the United Nations in New York City on July 8, 2004 to learn whether the UN possessed a copy of the "alleged fax or cable of January 10/11, 1994 supposedly sent from General Dallaire to Kofi Annan and others at UN HQ in New York...?" As Ralph Zacklin, the acting legal counsel in the UN's Office of Legal Counsel, replied to Black on August 11: "[W]e are providing you with a copy of a fax dated 11 January 1994 from General Dallaire to General Baril of DPKO that seems to match the description of the document provided in your letter. The United Nations has *not been able to locate the original of this document.*"[265]

That is to say, the copy of the document that the United Nations *was* able to locate and the copy of it that Zacklin's Office of Legal Counsel faxed to Christopher Black is the one we're calling Copy C: The November 27, 1995 Connaughton Fax. It is only when stripped of the three clusters of information we have reviewed above that the Connaughton Fax becomes the "Genocide Fax" (Copy A and Copy B). So why strip the Connaughton Fax of these three clusters of information?

The reason is simple: The need to pretend that the Connaughton Fax isn't the Connaughton Fax, but rather the original January 11, 1994 code cable that Dallaire allegedly sent to Baril at the DPKO in New York City. Otherwise, there is no "Genocide Fax," only a fax that features protecting an informant who claimed knowledge of weapons caches belonging to the MRND (*Mouvement Républicain National pour la Démocratie et le Développement*, the political party of Rwanda's then President Juvénal Habyarimana). Exactly as the Khan-initiated search of the DPKO's files had determined as far back as early November 1995 ("there was no information or indication of planned genocide"), reiterated by Zacklin in his fax to Black on August 11, 2004 ("The United Nations has not been able to locate the original of this document"). Enter the Connaughton Fax, but with the vital information identifying its November 27, 1995 origin in Camberley, Surrey, and the November 28, 1995 annotation by Lamin J. Sise, both removed from it, so as to disguise its true origin and to pretend that it is the original Dallaire code cable dated January 11, 1994.

In conclusion, the document that is referred to as the "Genocide Fax," which claims that on January 11, 1994, UNAMIR Force Commander Roméo Dallaire "reported in startling detail the preparations that were underway to carry out precisely such an extermination campaign," as Philip Gourevitch described it back in1998,[266] ought to be renamed the *Connaughton Fax*, accorded zero credibility on the question of an alleged Hutu plot to exterminate the country's Tutsi, and be permanently withdrawn from all documentary histories related to Rwanda 1994.

Notes

Introduction

1 We carried out three Factiva database searches under the combined "Wires," "Newspapers: All," and "Transcripts" categories on May 2, 2014 , for the periods April 6 – 8, April 1 – 14, and January 1 - April 30, 2014. Our search parameters were: *rst=(twir or tnwp or ttpt) and rwanda* w/10 genocid**. The results were as follows: April 6 – 8: 1,380 items; April 1 – 14: 2,638 items; and January 1 – April 30, 2014: 6,444 items.

2 Nicholas Watt, "Syria crisis: failure to intervene will have terrible consequences, says Blair," *The Guardian*, April 8, 2014.
< http://tinyurl.com/qjy3nqq >

3 Michael Dobbs, "Rwanda's Shrouded Nightmare," *New York Times*, January 10, 2014.—For the record, although it is clear that Dobbs believes that genocide was planned, he was savagely attacked for writing that the issue "has been hotly debated by scholars, politicians and lawyers." See Sections 10 and 11, below.
< http://tinyurl.com/k2ze336 >

4 Michael Dobbs, "Genocide Fax," Parts I – VI, United States Holocaust Memorial Museum, 2014. < http://tinyurl.com/pgdgnrk >.

5 Michael Dobbs, "The Rwanda 'Genocide Fax': What We Know Now," Electronic Briefing Book No. 452, The National Security Archive, January 9, 2014. < http://tinyurl.com/l7p3yl6 >.

6 See "Rwanda 20 Years Later," United States Holocaust Memorial Museum, 2014. < http://tinyurl.com/pf2ge7j >.

7 See Philip Gourevitch, "The Genocide Fax," *The New Yorker*, May 11, 1998. < http://tinyurl.com/lxbff7t >

8 "Reflections on the Genocide in Rwanda 20 Years Later," United States Holocaust Memorial Museum, March 18, 2014.
< http://tinyurl.com/kfo3qrf >

9 See "2014 Elie Wiesel Award," United States Holocaust Memorial Museum, April 30, 2014. < http://tinyurl.com/kvf9sp2 >

10 See, e.g., David Rieff, *Slaughterhouse: Bosnia and the Failure of the West* (New York: Simon & Shuster, 1995).

11 Although the Rwanda Patriotic Front is a political organization, and its armed wing from 1990 through July 1994 was known as the Rwandan Patriotic Army, to simplify matters, throughout our analysis, we will use the phrase Rwandan Patriotic Front (or RPF) to refer to both entities. However, after the RPF took power in July 1994, the Rwandan Patriotic Army became the name of the national armed forces of Rwanda. Then in 2002, the Rwandan Patriotic Army was renamed the Rwanda Defense Force. For more on this, see the website of Rwanda's Ministry of Defense. < http://tinyurl.com/oxxbgbk >

12 See Filip Reyntjens, *Political Governance in Post-Genocide Rwanda* (New York: Cambridge University Press, 2013), especially Ch. 1-3, pp. 1-97.

13 See Philip Gourevitch, *We wish to inform you that tomorrow we will be killed with our families: Stories from Rwanda* (New York: Picador, 1998), pp. 225-226.

14 Reyntjens, *Political Governance in Post-Genocide Rwanda*, p. xiii, quoting a prepared statement by the Clinton Foundation as Paul Kagame received its 2009 Global Citizens Award, September 23, 2009.

15 "Elie Wiesel and President Paul Kagame in the Great Hall," Cooper Union, New York City, September 30, 2013.
< http://tinyurl.com/mjlf2jw >.

16 "President Kagame attends Milken Institute Global Conference," Los Angeles, Office of the President of Rwanda, April 28, 2014.
< http://tinyurl.com/mfny9sx >

1. Rwanda: Background and context

17 William H. Draper III, *Human Development Report 1991* (New York: United Nations Development Program, 1991), p. iii. The 1991 report covered the calendar year 1990. Its interpretation of current history was at best embarrassingly quaint. < http://tinyurl.com/osayf3y >

18 On July 25, 1959, Rwanda's long-serving Tutsi King Mutara Rudahigwa died. His successor, the young Tutsi King Kigeri Ndahindurwa, was deposed in early 1960. All of Rwanda's kings had been

Tutsi. Ndahindurwa was Rwanda's last king. (See Arial Sabar, "A King With No Country," *The Washingtonian*, March 27, 2013.) < http://tinyurl.com/cr2qg22 >

19 See Catharine Newbury, *The Cohesion of Oppression: Citizenship and Ethnicity in Rwanda, 1860 – 1960* (New York: Columbia University Press, 1988), especially Ch. 3, "State and Society under Rwabugiri," pp. 38-52. Also see Mahmood Mamdani, *When Victims Become Killers: Colonialism, Nativism, and the Genocide in Rwanda* (Princeton NJ: Princeton University Press, 2001), especially Ch. 2, "The Origins of Hutu and Tutsi," pp. 41-75.

20 *Ibid.*, p. 75.—As Catharine Newbury explains the genesis of the modern political identities of "Hutu" and "Tutsi" within Rwanda: "The state-building efforts of [King] Rwabugiri [1860-1895] heightened awareness of ethnic differences….[L]ines of distinction were altered and sharpened, as the categories of Hutu and Tuutsi [her spelling] assumed new hierarchical overtones associated with proximity to the central court—proximity to power. Later, when the political arena widened and the intensity of political activity increased, these classifications became increasingly stratified and rigidified. More than simply conveying the connotation of cultural difference from Tuutsi, Hutu identity came to be associated with and eventually defined by inferior status….[T]he political salience of membership in one ethnic category or another came to depend on power….Under Rwabugiri, Tuutsi and Hutu became political labels; 'ethnicity', such as it was, came to assume a political importance, determining a person's life chances and relations with the authorities. With the establishment of European colonial rule in the country, ethnic categories came to be even more rigidly defined, while the disadvantages of being Hutu and the advantages of being Tuutsi increased significantly. Passing from one ethnic category to another was not impossible, but over time it became exceedingly difficult and, consequently, very rare." (Newbury, *The Cohesion of Oppression*, pp. 51-52.)

21 *Ibid.*, especially Ch. 9, "Pre-Independence Politics and Protests," pp. 180-206; here p. 191. As Gérard Prunier observes: "[T]he reality [the *Manifesto*] referred to, namely the humiliation and socio-economic inferiority of the Hutu community, could not be doubted." (*The*

Rwanda Crisis: History of a Genocide (New York: Columbia University Press, 1995), p. 45.)

22 Newbury, *The Cohesion of Oppression*, p. 193.

23 *Ibid.*, p. 187.

24 Prunier, *The Rwanda Crisis*, p. 49.

25 Newbury, *The Cohesion of Oppression*, p. 198.

26 According to Prunier: "The reason for letting Kayibanda starve rather than killing him seems to have been President Habyarimana's superstitious fear that his blood oath of fidelity to the former head of state would cause him harm if he actually shed the blood of the ex-President." (Prunier, *The Rwanda Crisis*, n. 72, p. 82.)

27 *Ibid.*, pp. 51-54.

28 See Ogenga Otunnu, "Rwandese Refugees and Immigrants in Uganda," in Howard Adelman and Astri Suhrke, Eds., *The Path of Genocide: The Rwandan Crisis from Uganda to Zaire* (New Brunswick, NJ: Transaction Publishers, 1999), Table 1.1, p. 9; and Table 1.4, p. 20.

29 Catharine Watson, *Exile from Rwanda: Background to an Invasion* (Washington D.C.: U.S. Committee for Refugees, February, 1991), p. 11. < http://tinyurl.com/mb3qqtt >

30 See Stephen Kinzer, *A Thousand Hills: Rwanda's Rebirth and the Man Who Dreamed It* (Hoboken, NJ: John Wiley & Sons, Inc., 2008), pp. 62-68. For the record, we regard Kinzer's book as a hagiography of Kagame Power, and Kinzer as a stenographer for the same. When we quote from his book, we do so with these caveats in mind.

31 In the overwhelming majority of the accounts of the RPF's October 1, 1990 invasion of Rwanda, the RPF's soldiers are treated as "deserters" or "defectors" from the Ugandan People's Defense Force, with the UPDF playing no role in the RPF's war. But this is false, and has always served as a cover story to hide the truth. In fact, the RPF was built-up within the UPDF with the full knowledge of President Museveni, and under UPDF Major General Fred Rwigyema, the RPF simply detached from the UPDF to carry out the invasion of Rwanda. When this initial invasion was badly defeated by the Armed Forces of Rwanda (with the crucial assistance of French, Belgian, and Zairean troops), and nearly destroyed in late 1990, the RPF retreated

to Uganda, where they reassembled, gathered new UPDF recruits, and were resupplied by the UPDF, as well as by the United States and Britain. The RPF re-launched its invasion of Rwanda under Paul Kagame's command on January 23, 1991. As Ogenga Otunnu has written, "The existing evidence...indicates that [Museveni's] regime trained, provided sanctuary, arms, logistical support, political, and diplomatic assistance to the [RPF] throughout the period of military engagement in Rwanda." ("An Historical Analysis of the Invasion by the Rwandan Patriotic Army (RPA)," in Adelman and Suhrke, Eds., *The Path of Genocide*, pp. 31-49; here p. 48. (Also see Ssemujju Ibrahim Nganda, "Open Secrets: Museveni's untold role in RPF war," *The Observer* [Kampala], July 8, 2009.) < http://tinyurl.com/pj7nkxk >

32 Kinzer, *A Thousand Hills*, p. 49.

33 Catharine Watson observes that, "Before the invasion, it was generally believed by close observers that most refugees, if offered a free choice to repatriate to Rwanda or remain (and someday naturalize) in Uganda, would actually chose the latter...." For Watson, this suggests that the "'refugee problem' could [have been] resolved with minimal actual repatriation." (Watson, *Exile from Rwanda*, p. 13.) Alas, the RPF never permitted this to happen. < http://tinyurl.com/mb3qqtt >

34 See the *Peace Agreement between the Government of the Republic of Rwanda and the Rwandese Patriotic Front*, signed at Arusha on August 4 1993, UN General Assembly (A/48/824-S/26915), December 23, 1993. A total of seven documents were gathered together as the "Arusha Accords," most notably the two *Protocols of Agreement between the Government of the Republic of Rwanda and the Rwandese Patriotic Front on Power-Sharing within the Framework of a Broad-Based Transitional Government*, October 30, 1992 and January 9, 1993, pp. 22-58; the *Protocol of Agreement between the Government of the Republic of Rwanda and the Rwandese Patriotic Front on the Repatriation of Rwandese Refugees and the Resettlement of Displaced Persons*, June 9, 1993, pp. 59-73; and the *Protocol of Agreement between the Government of the Republic of Rwanda and the Rwandese Patriotic Front on the Integration of the Armed Forces of the Two Parties*, August 3, 1993, pp. 74-173. < http://tinyurl.com/qcew5fa >

35 *Protocol...on the Integration of the Armed Forces of the Two Parties*, Article 74, pp. 117-119. < http://tinyurl.com/qcew5fa >

36 Robin Philpot, *Rwanda and the New Scramble for Africa: From Tragedy to Useful Imperial Fiction* (Montréal: Baraka Books, 2013), pp. 58-60.

37 Prunier, *The Rwanda Crisis*, p. 199.

38 "Burundi Refugees and Displaced Persons: Fact Sheet," U.S. Department of State, March 14, 1994, p. 1. < http://tinyurl.com/q3n76ju > Also see Kristin Scalzo, Ed., "The Rwandan Refugee Crisis: Before the Genocide," Electronic Briefing Book No. 464, The National Security Archive, March 31, 2014. < http://tinyurl.com/kfd2jol >

39 According to UNAMIR Force Commander Roméo Dallaire, as of September 1993, "It [was] estimated that, out of the original 900,000 [internally displaced people in Rwanda], 350,000 [had] not yet returned home." In Peter Erlinder, Ed., *Report of the UN Reconnaissance Mission to Rwanda—August 1993* (Saint Paul, MN: International Humanitarian Law Institute, 2011), p. 16.

40 U.S. Ambassador Robert A. Flaten, Kigali, Cable No. 1993Kigali 03970, November 4, 1993, para. 8, p. 5 (as posted by to the website of the National Security Archive). < http://tinyurl.com/k48awhn >

41 René Lemarchand, *Burundi: Ethnic Conflict and Genocide* (New York: Cambridge University Press, 2nd Ed., 1996), p. xiv. Also see Ch. 5, "The 1972 watershed," pp. 76-105; especially pp. 96-105.

42 Roméo Dallaire, *Shake Hands with the Devil: The Failure of Humanity in Rwanda* (Toronto: Vintage Canada, 2004), p. 98.

43 Prunier, *The Rwanda Crisis*, n. 15, p. 202.

44 N.A., "Burundi: Implications of the Coup," U.S. Department of State, October 29, 1993, reproduced in Peter Erlinder, *The Accidental... Genocide* (Saint Paul, MN: International Humanitarian Law Institute, 2013), p. 112. As Erlinder himself adds: "[T]he Burundian example, itself, demonstrated that the Tutsi military violently rejected majority-rule elections and engaged in mass killings of the Hutu majority, which must certainly have reinforced the deep-seated fear of Tutsi domination..." (*Ibid.*, pp. 108-109). < http://tinyurl.com/k2opuat >

45 *Protocol...on the Integration of the Armed Forces of the Two Parties*, Article 72, p 116. < http://tinyurl.com/qcew5fa >

46 Dallaire, *Shake Hands with the Devil*, pp. 126-127; pp. 130-131.

2. The RPF invasion and low-level aggressive war that never was a "civil war"

47 In Erlinder, Ed., *Report of the UN Reconnaissance Mission to Rwanda—August 1993*, pp. 35-38.

48 *Ibid.*, pp. 39-40.

49 The RPF's military superiority over the FAR and other government forces (e.g., the Gendarmerie, the Para-Commando Battalion, and the Presidential Guard) is argued at length in Erlinder, *The Accidental... Genocide, passim.* < http://tinyurl.com/k2opuat >

50 According to William Cyrus Reed, "When the RPF invaded Rwanda in 1990 it had 36 cells inside the country, with nine in Kigali and others in Kigongi, Butare, Gitarama, and Byumba, albeit so clandestine that out of the 8,000-10,000 arrested that year only three were members.... Two years later, however, following the regime's recognition of the RPF, cells emerged once again, and by August 1993 the number in Kigali alone had grown to 146...." ("Exile, Reform, and the Rise of the Rwandan Patriotic Front," *The Journal of Modern African Studies*, Vol. 34, No. 3 (1996), p. 496.)

51 Here we are drawing on the superb research of Christian Davenport and Allan Stam *et al.*, specifically their videographic "Animation of Battle Fronts & Conflict Zones," GenoDynamics.
< http://tinyurl.com/maoaak2 >

52 Dallaire, *Shake Hands with the Devil*, p. 288.

53 *Ibid.*, p. 299.

54 See UN Security Council Resolution 827 (S/RES/827), May 25, 1993.
< http://tinyurl.com/o2l2cx5 >

55 See UN Security Council Resolution 955 (S/RES/955), November 8, 1994. < http://tinyurl.com/lljyu9n >

56 Richard J. Goldstone, *First Amended Indictment, The Prosecutor of the Tribunal against Clement Kayishema et al.*, Case No. ICTR-95-1-I, International Criminal Tribunal for Rwanda, April 19, 1995, para. 19, emphasis added. < http://tinyurl.com/oktx76c >

57 Bernard Muna, *Indictment*, *The Prosecutor v. Jean Kambanda*, Case No. ICTR-97-23-DP, October 16, 1997, para. 3.4, emphasis added. < http://tinyurl.com/mgof26n >

58 Bernard A. Muna, *Amended Indictment*, *The Prosecutor against Theoneste Bagosora*, Case No.ICTR-96-7-I, International Criminal Tribunal for Rwanda, December 8, 1999, para. 2.5, emphasis added. < http://tinyurl.com/lz9ct27 >

59 See R.W. Apple, Jr., "The Iraq Invasion," *New York Times*, August 3, 1990. Also see "Iraq's Naked Aggression," Editorial, *New York Times*, August 3, 1990.

60 "The Commission finds itself obliged to conclude that there have been acts of genocide, as contemplated by international law. In this respect, the responsibility of the head of state and of his immediate entourage, including members of his family, is the inescapable conclusion." This quote derives from the "English Summary" of the *Rapportt de la Commission Internationale d'Enquete sur les Violations des droits de l'Homme au Rwanda depuis le 1er Octobre 1990 (7 – 21 janvier 1993)*, March, 1993, p. 6. < http://tinyurl.com/khuxry3 >

61 The earliest use of the term 'genocide' in the English-language media that we've ever been able to find to describe the situation in Rwanda was in a March 24, 1992 Reuters report: "'The Tutsi are being systematically massacred...This is genocide', Andre Jadoul, a Belgian lawyer who has been on two recent observer missions to Rwanda, told a news conference in Paris." (William Emmanuel, "Rwandan Opposition Accuses Government of Genocide," Reuters, March 24, 1992.)

62 Allain Pellet, Ed., "The Opinions of the Badinter Arbitration Committee: A Second Breath for the Self-Determination of Peoples," *European Journal of International Law*, Vol. 3, No. 1, 1992, Opinion No. 1, para. 3. < http://tinyurl.com/obz6zmv > Also see Danilo Turk, Ed., "Opinions No. 4-10 of the Arbitration Commission of the International Conference on Yugoslavia...," *European Journal of International Law*, Vol. 4, No. 1, 1993. < http://tinyurl.com/nt4q3sh >

63 In Marlise Simons, "War Crimes Trial Seeks to Define the Balkan Conflict," *New York Times*, May 12, 1996. < http://tinyurl.com/ok4j5l5 >

64 See the file on Dusko Tadić, "Prijedor," Case No. IT-94-1, Interna-

tional Criminal Tribunal for the Former Yugoslavia.
< http://tinyurl.com/kv3oyjx > Especially see the testimony by defense witness Robert Hayden, September 10, 1996.
< http://tinyurl.com/n76lsve >, and September 11, 1996.
< http://tinyurl.com/m7ser4s >

3. "Hutu Power extremists" did not shoot-down Habyarimana's Falcon 50 jet

65 Dobbs, "Rwanda's Shrouded Nightmare."
< http://tinyurl.com/k2ze336 >
66 Prunier, *The Rwanda Crisis*, p. 221. Prunier called this the "most probable hypothesis" (p. 221). Prunier's account contains serious errors; today it reads more like a fossil of the standard model than it did when first published—and, we might add, that although Prunier is a very fine historian of Africa's Great Lakes region, the moment that he takes-up the topic of the "Rwandan genocide," he reverts to a strict standard-modeler. For example, Prunier asserted that "it was not in the political interest of the RPF to kill President Habyarimana." And shortly thereafter, that "if the RPF had planned to kill President Habyarimana, it would have been prepared to leap forward militarily. This was not at all the case. The Falcon 50 was shot down in the evening of April 6 and there was no RPF reaction" (p. 220). But the RPF did leap forward militarily as soon as Kagame received the report of the successful shoot-down at his headquarters in Mulindi. Moreover, the names of the actual RPF shooters as well as those involved in the planning have been divulged by RPF exiles and circulated in critical circles for years.
67 Resolution 955 (S/RES/955), para. 1. < http://tinyurl.com/lljyu9n >
68 *Affidavit of Michael Andrew Hourigan*, March 8, 2007 (as posted to the website of the Rwanda Documents Project, No. DNT 365).
< http://tinyurl.com/kzy97r2 > Hourigan's affidavit was entered into the evidentiary record at the Military I trial of the Para-Commando Battalion leader Major Aloys Ntabakuze by his lead counsel, the American defense attorney Peter Erlinder. The Hourigan affair has

been so successfully redacted from the standard model of the "Rwandan genocide" that his name does not turn up even once in Human Right Watch's massive 800-page *Leave None To Tell the Story*. (See n. 102, below.) When Hourigan died suddenly in early December 2013 at his home in Adelaide, Australia, his death went unmentioned by the U.S., British, and Canadian media. Also see the interview that ICTR defense attorney John Philpot conducted with Hourigan at the Second International Criminal Defense Conference, held in Brussels on May 21-23, 2010, "Louise Arbour Was Wrong."
< http://vimeo.com/12025909 >

69 See the "Prepared Statement of Mr. James R. Lyons," April 6, 2001, reproduced in Erlinder, *The Accidental... Genocide*, pp. 49-51.
< http://tinyurl.com/k2opuat > A former FBI counter-terrorism agent, Lyons was Commander of Investigations at the ICTR during the time of the Hourigan investigation, and Lyons was present in the room with Hourigan when Arbour ordered Hourigan to shut-down his investigation of the assassination. Lyons corroborates Hourigan's account of their meeting. < http://tinyurl.com/ndy7b56 >

70 Judge Jean-Louis Bruguière, *Request for the Issuance of International Arrest Warrants, Tribunal de Grande Instance*, Paris, France, November 21, 2006, p. 11. The nine RPF figures mentioned were: James Kabarebe, Kayumba Nyamwasa, Charles Kayonga, Jack Nziza, Samuel Kanyemere, Rose Kabuye, Jacob Tumwine, Frank Nziza, Eric Hakizamana (pp. 46-48). Paul Kagame, notably absent from this list of indictees, "enjoys the immunity granted in France to incumbent Heads of State and therefore cannot be prosecuted within the framework of this proceeding" (p. 46). (English Translation:
< http://tinyurl.com/kas5n57 >.)

71 *Ibid.*, p. 12.

72 According to ICTR defense attorney Peter Erlinder, "The total number of former RPF officers who have confessed in court proceedings or in public to RPF involvement in the Habyarimana assassination plot now exceeds eight (8), ranging from members of the missile crew to generals and Kagame's Chief of Staff [Theogene Rudasingwa]." (Erlinder, *The Accidental... Genocide*, n. 49, p. 25.) We suspect that the number may even be higher. < http://tinyurl.com/k2opuat >

73 Bruguière, *Request for the Issuance of International Arrest Warrants*, p. 17.

74 *Ibid.*, p. 19.

75 "Prepared Statement of Mr. James R. Lyons," in Erlinder, *The Accidental... Genocide*, p. 50. < http://tinyurl.com/k2opuat > Also see Bruguière, *Request for the Issuance of International Arrest Warrants*, p. 16. < http://tinyurl.com/kas5n57 >

76 In Reyntjens, *Political Governance in Post-Genocide Rwanda*, p. 10.

77 See David Smith, "Exiled Rwandan general attacks Paul Kagame as 'dictator'," *The Guardian*, July 30, 2012.
< http://tinyurl.com/pzguqbm > Also see Geoffrey York and Judi Rever, "Rwanda's hunted: Inside the plots to kill Rwanda's dissidents," *Toronto Globe and Mail*, May 3, 2014.
< http://tinyurl.com/ordt8o5 >

78 Theogene Rudasingwa, *Healing A Nation: A Testimony* (North Charleston, SC: CreateSpace Independent Publishing Platform, 2013), p. 150.

79 See *Rwanda: The Preventable Genocide*, International Panel of Eminent Personalities. Gerald Caplan was a member of the Secretariat, and is credited with having been this report's principal author.
< http://tinyurl.com/lvrotjb >

80 *Ibid.*, p. 270.

81 *Ibid.*, para. 9.14, p. 62.

82 *Ibid.*, p. 267.

83 Gerald Caplan, "Who killed the president of Rwanda?" *Pambazuka News*, January 21, 2010. < http://tinyurl.com/mjqkqvz >

84 For the RPF's self-inquiry into the shootdown of Habyarimana's presidential jet (i.e., the Independent Committee of Experts or Mutsinzi Committee, named after the titular head of the inquiry, Jean Mutsinzi), see *Report of the Investigation into the Causes and Circumstances of and Responsibility for the Attack of 06/04/1994 against the Falcon 50 Presidential Aeroplane, Registration Number 9XR-NN*, Independent Committee of Experts Charged with the Investigation into the Crash on 06/04/1994/...*, Kigali, Republic of Rwanda, January, 2010.
< http://tinyurl.com/mjgf8rn >

85 Similarly with *The New Yorker*'s Philip Gourevitch, who found the

RPF's self-inquiry an "extraordinary historical and political document," providing "remarkably convincing detail," and showing the "thoroughness and seriousness of the underlying investigation." Gourevitch's exercise in Kagame-Power flattery continued: The "report on Habyarimana's plane is the latest in a yearlong string of diplomatic and political moves that show the new Rwandan government achieving a level of sophistication, skill, and effectiveness in commanding international respect that has rarely, if ever, been seen before in Africa. A year ago, Rwanda was being blamed for all the woes of the war next door in the Democratic Republic of Congo—and now those woes have come to be seen overwhelmingly as the result of the continued presence of fugitive Hutu *génocidaires* in Congo. Leaders of these Hutu Power armies in exile, who had operated with impunity from European capitals, are being rounded up. And this week, on the day that the report first leaked in the French press, France's foreign minister, Bernard Kouchner, was in Kigali to announce the establishment of a special court in France to prosecute refugees suspected of genocide. Today's issue of Rwanda's official newspaper, *New Times*, announces that Sarkozy will visit next month." (Philip Gourevitch, "The Mutsinzi Report on the Rwandan Genocide," *The New Yorker*, January 8, 2010.) < http://tinyurl.com/y8mgs9z >

86 Filip Reyntjens, *A Fake Inquiry of a Major Event. Analysis of the Mutsinzi report on the 6th April 1994 attack on the Rwandan President's aeroplane*, Institute of Development Policy and Management, Working Paper 2010.07, University of Antwerp, 2010, p. 27. < http://tinyurl.com/llkq3tq > For an additional critique of the Mutsinzi report, see Luc Marchal *et al.*, "Analysis of the Mutsinzi Report," *CirqueMinime*, February 8, 2010. < http://tinyurl.com/os9duo2 > A Belgian soldier, Marchal served as the Belgian Contingent Commander in UNAMIR until Belgium withdrew its troops in April 1994.

87 Linda Melvern, "Expert Refutes Bruguiere Claims," *All Africa*, November 27, 2006. < http://tinyurl.com/ppenvrh >

88 Linda Melvern, "The Perfect Crime," *Prospect*, January 31, 2008, emphasis added. < http://tinyurl.com/k2plolh >

4. The "Rwandan genocide" by the numbers

89 Muna, *Indictment, The Prosecutor v. Jean Kambanda*, para. 3.20, p. 5. < http://tinyurl.com/mgof26n >

90 Ingvar Carlsson *et al.*, *Independent inquiry into the actions of the United Nations during the 1999 genocide in Rwanda* (S/1999/1257), United Nations, December 16, 1999, p. 3.
< http://tinyurl.com/kddoehn >

91 Christophe Bazivamo *et al.*, *Denombrement des Victimes du Genocide: Rapport Final* (Kigali: Ministere de l'Administration Locale, du Developpement Communautaire et des Affaires Sociales, April, 2004), Section 2.1, "Effectifs déclarés et Effectifs dénombrés" ("The numbers claimed and the actual numbers"), p. 21.
< http://tinyurl.com/p2k4gvw >

92 See Edwin Musoni, "Report claims 2 million killed in 1994 Genocide," *The New Times*, October 4, 2008. According to Musoni, the "President of the National Commission against Genocide, Jean de Dieu Mucyo, said that the figures in the [Genocide Survivors Students Association] report are not yet official and that his commission will have to verify the figures before regarding them as real." This observation was charitable of Mucyo indeed. < http://tinyurl.com/n797mak >

93 See the website, *Understanding Rwandan Political Violence in 1994*, GenoDynamics, < http://tinyurl.com/l8mxguy >, specifically the section titled "Data on Violence in 1994." < http://tinyurl.com/lfnvkff >

94 Christian Davenport and Allan Stam, *Rwandan Political Violence in Space and Time*, unpublished manuscript, 2004, especially pp. 27-33. < http://tinyurl.com/ntdrgqs > Also see their videographic display of RPF troop movements and violent deaths for the period April 1 – July 31, 1994, "Animation of Violent Deaths and Troop Overlays—Median Estimates," GenoDynamics. < http://tinyurl.com/kw6qpyu > As they wrote in 2009, summing-up what this videographic shows: "When the RPF advanced, large-scale killings escalated. When the RPF stopped, large-scale killings largely decrease." (Davenport and Stam, "What Really Happened in Rwanda?" *Miller-McCune*, October 6, 2009. < http://tinyurl.com/lpjan8o >) As we have argued elsewhere, we do not accept their conclusions concerning the responsi-

bility for the deaths they've documented, i.e., FAR versus RPF. Nevertheless, theirs is very important work. (See Edward S. Herman and David Peterson, *The Politics of Genocide* (New York: Monthly Review Press, 2nd Ed., 2011), "Rwanda and the Democratic Republic of Congo," pp. 51-68; here pp. 58-59.)

95 See David Peterson, "Rwanda's 1991 Census," ZBlogs, March 12, 2014. < http://tinyurl.com/lytftt6 >

96 See the "Statistics" webpage at the website of the U.K.-based Survivors Fund, n. 4. < http://tinyurl.com/mqvp82q >

97 See "Data on Violence in 1994," GenoDynamics.
< http://tinyurl.com/lfnvkff >

5. The West's alleged "falure to intervene"

98 Statement by Samantha Power, *Threats to international peace and security: Prevention and fight against genocide* (S/PV.7155), UN Security Council, April 16, 2014, p. 12.
< http://tinyurl.com/mo6mkco >.

99 *Ibid.*, p. 6.

100 Massimo Calabresi, "Susan Rice: A Voice for Intervention," *Time Magazine*, March 24, 2011. < http://tinyurl.com/q35m4jj >.

101 Samantha Power, *A Problem from Hell: America and the Age of Genocide* (New York: Basic Books, 2002), pp. 334-335.—In her Preface to the same book, Power writes that "Washington led a successful effort to remove most of the peacekeepers under [Gen. Dallaire's] command and then aggressively worked to block authorization of UN reinforcements" (p. xx). The reasonable inference from the fact that Washington removed peacekeepers and then blocked their reinforcement, to the fact that Washington wanted Kagame's RFP to seize state power, as it did, is inconceivable to Power. Her United States just does not behave this way.

102 Alison Des Forges *et al.*, *"Leave None To Tell the Story": Genocide in Rwanda* (New York: Human Rights Watch, 1999), p. 27.

103 As Herman J. Cohen, at the time the U.S. Assistant Secretary of State in charge of African Affairs, once asked: "[Why] did [the United

States] automatically exclude the policy option of informing Ugandan President Museveni that the invasion of Rwanda by uniformed members of the Ugandan army was totally unacceptable, and that the continuation of good relations between the United States and Uganda would depend on his getting the RPF back across the border?" The answer is of course too obvious for Cohen to recognize it. (Herman J. Cohen, *Intervening in Africa: Superpower Peacemaking in a Troubled Continent* (New York: St. Martin's Press, 2000), pp. 178-179.)

104 Erlinder, *The Accidental Genocide*, pp. 113-150.
< http://tinyurl.com/k2opuat >

105 See, e.g., Gerald Gahima and Claude Dusaidi, Statement by the Political Bureau of the Rwandese Patriotic Front on the Proposed Deployment of a U.N. Intervention Force in Rwanda, New York City, April 30, 1994 (as archived at the Rwanda Documents Project), p. 4. < http://tinyurl.com/qdj7mhq >

106 Dallaire, *Shake Hands with the Devil*, p. 364.

107 *Ibid.*, p. 364.

108 "Rwandan embassy closed, U.S. seeks to remove Rwanda from UN Council," Agence France Presse, July 15, 1994; "Clinton Orders Nonstop Aid Flights for Rwandan Victims," Associated Press, July 22, 1994; "U.S. recognizes new government in Rwanda," Reuters, July 29, 1994; "200 U.S. troops going into Kigali to open airport," Reuters, July 29, 1994.

109 George E. Moose, Memorandum drafted sometime between September 17 and 20, 1994, U.S. Department of State. In Erlinder, *The Accidental... Genocide*, pp. 311-312. < http://tinyurl.com/k2opuat >

6. The ICTR delivers victor's justice

110 Resolution 955 (S/RES/955), para. 1. < http://tinyurl.com/nlnh7yx >

111 See Judge Almiro Rodrigues *et al.*, *Judgment, Prosecutor v. Radislav Krstić*, Case No. IT-98-33-T, International Criminal Tribunal for the Former Yugoslavia, August 2, 2001, Section III G.2, "Mens rea," para. 544-599. "The Chamber concludes that the intent to kill all

the Bosnian Muslim men of military age in Srebrenica constitutes an intent to destroy in part the Bosnian Muslim group…and therefore must be qualified as genocide" (para. 598).

< http://tinyurl.com/lohd5hy > Also see Judge Theodor Meron *et al.*, *Judgment on Appeal, Prosecutor v Radislav Krstić*, Case No. IT-98-33-A, International Criminal Tribunal for the Former Yugoslavia, April 19, 2004, Section II, "The Trial Chamber's Finding that Genocide Occurred in Srebrenica," para. 1-38.

< http://tinyurl.com/lm7mpv2 >

112 See Judge Mohamed Shahabuddeen *et al.*, *Decision on Prosecutor's Interlocutory Appeal of Decision on Judicial Notice, Prosecutor v. Edouard Karemera et al.*, Case No. ICTR-98-44-AR73(C), June 16, 2006. < http://tinyurl.com/ka45avz >

113 John Laughland, "Destroying the rule of law," Sanders Research Associates (as posted to the CirqueMinimie website), July 6, 2006. < http://tinyurl.com/o9xdnaj >

114 Resolution 955 (S/RES/955), para. 1. < http://tinyurl.com/nlnh7yx >

115 Statement by Manzi Bakuramutsa, *The situation concerning Rwanda*, UN Security Council (S/PV.3453), November 8, 1994, pp. 14-15. < http://tinyurl.com/kfn7y3n >

116 Reyntjens, *Political Governance in Post-Genocide Rwanda*, p. 244.

117 Linda Melvern, *Conspiracy to Murder: The Rwandan Genocide* (New York: Verso, Rev. Ed., 2006), p. 2.

118 Judge Laïty Kama *et al.*, *Judgment and Sentence, The Prosecutor versus Jean Kambanda*, Case No.: ICTR 97-23-S, International Criminal Tribunal for Rwanda, September 4, 1998, para. 42(2). < http://tinyurl.com/ojm8b77 >

119 *Ibid.*, para. 39(i-ii).

120 Reyntjens, *Political Governance in Post-Genocide Rwanda*, p. 242. Also see John Laughland, *A History of Political Trials from Charles I to Saddam Hussein* (Oxford: Peter Lang, 2008), Ch. 16, "Jean Kambanda, Convicted without Trial," pp. 207-220.

121 Kama *et al.*, *Judgment and Sentence, The Prosecutor versus Jean Kambanda*, para. 40(1).

122 Melvern, *Conspiracy to Murder*, p. 1. In contrast, Reyntjens quotes the French journalist Thierry Cruvellier, who wrote that by "avoiding

a trial, thanks to the [plea] agreement concluded between the defendant and the prosecutor, the Tribunal thus nourished a judicial fiction." (Reyntjens, *Political Governance in Post-Genocide Rwanda*, p. 242.)

123 "War crimes prosecutor hails Rwandan judgments," Agence France Presse, September 4, 1998.

124 Laughland, *A History of Political Trials*, pp. 218-219.—Laughland also quotes a September 2003 letter that Kamdanda released from his prison cell at Bamako, Mali. As Kambanda wrote: "In virtue of the fact that the massacres had been going on for three days, it is impossible that the government I led could have planned them. Its members had nothing in common ideologically…all planning between the parties was impossible. At no point, during my time in office as prime minister, did I have any knowledge of the conception or any plan for these massacres, neither before nor after the assassination of President Habyarimana. I would have known about this since I had the Central Intelligence Service under my supervision. Without the assassination of President Habyarimana, interethnic massacres on this scale would definitely not have taken place. It is therefore essential to find those responsible for that attack and he or they must be held responsible for the consequences of their crime." (*Ibid.*, p. 219.)

125 See Carla Del Ponte, with Chuck Sudetic, *Madame Prosecutor: Confrontations with Humanity's Worst Criminals and the Culture of Impunity: A Memoir* (New York: Other Press, 2009), Ch. 7, "Confronting Kigali 2000 to 2001," pp. 177-192; and especially Ch. 9, "Confronting Kigali 2002 and 2003," pp. 223-241. Also see Peter Erlinder, "The Rwanda War Crimes Coverup," *Global Research*, September 3, 2009. < http://tinyurl.com/o7z5jk5 >

126 Chris McGreal, "Genocide tribunal ready to indict first Tutsis," *The Guardian*, April 5, 2002. < http://tinyurl.com/ooga7sf >

127 Chris McGreal, "Witness boycott brings Rwandan genocide trials to a halt," *The Guardian*, July 29, 2002. < http://tinyurl.com/kh36m5p >

128 Column Lynch, "U.N. Official Criticizes Rwanda," *Washington Post*, July 25, 2002. < http://tinyurl.com/mdxntnk >

129 Del Ponte and Sudetic, *Madame Prosecutor*, p. 233.

130 Kofi Annan, *Letter dated 28 July 2003 from the Secretary-General addressed to the President of the Security Council* (S/2003/766), July 28, 2003. < http://tinyurl.com/mkc2hor >

131 UN Security Council Resolution 1503 (S/RES/1503), August 28, 2003, para. 8 and Annex I. < http://tinyurl.com/ky669wz >

132 After her termination as chief prosecutor at the ICTR, Del Ponte was asked by an interviewer what she would have done, had she been given the choice to remain the chief prosecutor at either the ICTR or the ICTY? Del Ponte replied: "I believe I would have opted for the ICTR because I still remain with one challenge: the special investigations." ("Interview with Carla Del Ponte: 'If I had had the choice, I would have remained prosecutor of the ICTR'," *The Arusha Times*, September 20-26, 2003.)
< http://tinyurl.com/kq3xds8 >

133 See, e.g., "General Ndindiliyimana demands that charges against him be dropped," Hirondelle News Agency, May 21, 2003. In the Military II trial chamber, Ndindiliyimana's defense attorney, the Canadian Christopher Black, argued that since "only members of the former Hutu majority regime in Rwanda are targeted for prosecution while Tutsis, belonging to the Rwandan Patriotic Front and its allies, who have committed similar war crimes as those alleged against the Hutus, including genocide, are granted effective immunity from prosecution," the prosecution's policy "has no legitimate criminal justice objective, only a political one."
< http://tinyurl.com/o3s7qll > For the ICTR's decision rejecting this complaint, see Judge Arlette Ramaroson *et al.*, *Decision on Urgent Oral Motion for a Stay of the Indictment, or in the Alternative a Reference to the Security Council, The Prosecutor v. Ndindilimana*, Case No. ICTR-2000-56-I, International Criminal Tribunal for Rwanda, March 26, 2004. < http://tinyurl.com/l7b79bx >

134 Hassan B. Jallow, "Prosecutorial Discretion and International Criminal Justice," *Journal of International Criminal Justice*, Vol. 3, No. 1, 2005, p. 156.

135 *Ibid.*, p. 150.

136 Philpot, *Rwanda and the New Scramble for Africa*, Ch. 13, "International Criminal Justice as 'Battering Ram'," pp. 175-193; here pp.

182-183.

7. The alleged Hutu "conspiracy to commit genocide" that never was

137 The crime of "genocide" is defined by the International Criminal Tribunal for Rwanda as "any of the following acts committed with intent to destroy, in whole or in part, a national, ethnical, racial or religious group, as such," followed by five specific qualifications: "(a) Killing members of the group; (b) Causing serious bodily or mental harm to members of the group; (c) Deliberately inflicting on the group conditions of life calculated to bring about its physical destruction in whole or in part; (d) Imposing measures intended to prevent births within the group; (e) Forcibly transferring children of the group to another group." (Statute of the International Criminal Tribunal for Rwanda, January, 2010, Article 2, "Genocide," p. 59.) < http://tinyurl.com/md4ftvg >

138 Atsu-Koffi Amega *et al.*, *Final Report of the Commission of Experts established pursuant to Security Council resolution 935 (1994)*, UN Security Council (S/1994/1405), December 9, 1994, para. 58. < http://tinyurl.com/qdqobn7 >

139 Muna, *Amended Indictment, The Prosecutor against Theoneste Bagosora*, para. 5.1. This section of the indictment is titled "Concise statement of the facts: Preparation." Continuing the same theme, Count 1 of this indictment states that Bagosora *et al.* "conspired… to kill and cause serious bodily or mental harm to members of the Tutsi population with the intent to destroy, in whole or in part, a racial or ethnic group, and thereby committed conspiracy to commit genocide…" (p. 54). < http://tinyurl.com/lz9ct27 >

140 Daniel Jonah Goldhagen, *Worse Than War: Genocide, Eliminationism, and the Onoing Assault on Humanity* (New York: Public Affairs, 2009), p. 288. Here we add the revealing fact that neither the names Paul Kagame nor Rwandan Patriotic Front appear even once in Goldhagen's 650-page tract. For Goldhagen, the events of April-July 1994 were the monocausal result the Hutu population's anti-Tutsi eliminationist and exterminationist beliefs.

141 According to the December 1999 Carlsson report, as early as April 13, 1994, the "RPF representative at the United Nations, Mr Claude Dusaidi, in his letter to the President of the Security Council, said that 'a crime of genocide' had been committed against the Rwandan people...." (Carlsson *et al.*, *Independent inquiry into the actions of the United Nations during the 1999 genocide in Rwanda*, p. 68.) < http://tinyurl.com/kddoehn >

142 See, e.g., the website of the Embassy of the United States, Kigali, Rwanda. < http://tinyurl.com/n96nj2g >

143 Namely, the trials of some of the highest-profile Hutu political and military command known as Government I (Édouard Karemera, Matthieu Ngirumpatse, Joseph Nzirorera (deceased), André Rwamakuba); Government II (Casimir Bizimungu, Justin Mugenzi, Jérôme-Clément Bicamumpaka, Prosper Mugiraneza); Military I (Théoneste Bagosora, Gratien Kabiligi, Aloys Ntabakuze, Anatole Nsengiyumva); and Military II (Augustin Ndindiliyimana, Augustin Bizimungu, François-Xavier Nzuwonemeye, Innocent Sagahutu).— See our "Appendix I: More on the alleged Hutu 'conspiracy to commit genocide' that never was."

144 To illustrate the dramatic use of gory detail by the African Rights report, consider the following passage, recounted by a young mother: "They ordered me to take [my son] Déo to a pit latrine. When we got there, I saw that it was already full of corpses. I was to kill him myself but I refused. I pleaded with those who would kill him to allow me to go away before they macheted him. After a few minutes, I saw them looking for hoes to put the soil on my son's body. They were boasting that 'The father was the first in the pit. Now, let the son act as the lid' [Jean-Paul] Birindabagabo then told me that he had not wanted my son killed, telling me that my own fate was to be decided soon." (Rakiya Omaar and Alex de Waal, *Rwanda: Death, Despair and Defiance* (London, African Rights, 1994), p. 347.) In short, the scene is so frankly gruesome, it must be taken as evidence of something far more encompassing—"The Genocide."

145 To better understand what we mean by the role of "riches of dramatic detail" in conveying the impression that everything is part of something far greater, namely, "The Genocide," consider the following

paragraph from Human Rights Watch's treatment of events in the Butare prefecture: "With the enormous instability introduced by the genocide, political actors at all levels jostled for power for themselves and their parties. At the prefectural level, MRND stalwarts Nyiramasuhuko and Kalimanzira struggled against the growth of MDR-Power represented by men like Semwaga. This struggle intensified towards the end of the genocide when Shalom, as head of the MRND Interahamwe, prepared attacks against the sector Gatobotobo of Mbazi, where Semwaga and Prefect Nsabimana were protecting Tutsi. The MRND group called RTLM to their assistance and the radio station broadcast information about the continued presence of Tutsi in that sector. Semwaga also previously fought challenges from a CDR leader, the former burgomaster of Mbazi, Kabuga, who [had] been one of the most zealous organizers of the genocide in that commune. According to local observers, Semwaga apparently was behind the abduction and murder of Kabuga and his associates like Masumbuko. Soldiers, including Sergeant Gatwaza, reportedly arrived one day in May to carry them off along with Emmanuel Sakindi, a councilor who was said to be Tutsi. The supposed Tutsi and the apparent killers of Tutsi were reportedly all killed by the same people at the same time, but for different reasons. Whether or not Sibomana, the burgomaster of Mbazi, participated in instigating the murder, as is sometimes charged, he benefited from the elimination of Kabuga, who had challenged his authority." (Des Forges *et al.*, *"Leave None To Tell the Story"*, p. 556.) As with the previous note, the passage is so detailed, it must be taken as evidence of something far more encompassing—"The Genocide."

146 See Robert Gersony, "Summary of UNHCR Presentation Before Commission of Experts," October 11, 1994 pp. 4-8. Gersony had been dispatched to Rwanda on behalf of the UN High Commissioner for Refugees' Emergency Repatriation Team, and he reported to the UN Commission of Experts in October, 1994. He told them that in several of Rwanda's prefectures he found an "unmistakable pattern" of "systematic and sustained killing and persecution of their civilian Hutu populations by the RPF," with between 5,000 and 10,000 Hutu killed per month since April. < http://tinyurl.com/lkxq9ze >

147 See Philpot, *Rwanda and the New Scramble for Africa*, Part 2, Ch. 8-12, pp. 131-171. "Any body of literature of this magnitude inevitably generates a set of conventions, images, and metaphors," Philpot writes. "[W]hen an image is constantly repeated, it becomes the substance itself. European ethnocentrism is the constant and unifying theme of this literary convention. 'Ethnocentrism created and preserved until today a persistent fantasy: the civilized Briton in confrontation with savage Africans in an Africa that never was'." (pp. 131-133.) Also see Johan Pottier, *Re-imaging Rwanda: Conflict, Survival and Disinformation in the Late Twentieth Century* (New York: Cambridge University Press, 2002). Here we'd add that since Rwanda's Hutu were as of 1994 official-enemy targets of the United States, Britain, the RPF, and human rights NGOs, the kind of literary conventions, images, and metaphors that Philpot describes would have been marshaled against the Hutu. And they still continue to be, 20 years later.

148 Thierry Cruvellier, "ICTR: Rwandan Genocide—no master plan," Radio Netherlands Worldwide, December 19, 2011.
< http://tinyurl.com/lyjr7e9 >

8. Did Paul Kagame's RPF really "stop the genocide"?

149 Des Forges *et al.*, *"Leave None to Tell the Story"*, p. 20.
150 Omaar and de Waal, *Rwanda*, p. 628.
151 Maria Malagardis, "Paul Kagame : 'Paris a été impliqué avant, pendant et après le génocide'," *Libération*, April 6, 2014.
< http://tinyurl.com/lvduhzx >
152 Dallaire, *Shake Hands with the Devil*, pp. 294-295. The event Dallaire describes here took place around mid-April.
153 Quoting Kagame, Dallaire writes: "If an intervention force is sent to Rwanda, we will fight it." (*Ibid.*, p. 342.)
154 Reyntjens, *Political Governance in Post-Genocide Rwanda*, p. 184.

9. "Africa's World War": Kagame's alleged pursuit of *"génocidaires"*

in Zaire—the Democratic Republic of Congo—and the deaths of millions

155 In this section, we will largely limit ourselves to the "first" war in Zaire-the Democratic Republic of Congo, *ca.* September 1996 through May 1997, and not the "second" war, which has lasted from August 1998 through the present day.

156 We adopt the convention of referring to Zaire for the period through May 1997, by which date Mobutu Sese Seko, Zaire's long-time ruler, had been overthrown and replaced by Laurent Désiré Kabila; and we will refer to the Democratic Republic of Congo for the period from the end of May 1997 on, at which time, Zaire was renamed the Democratic Republic of Congo.

157 The origin of phrases such as "Africa's first World War" and "first African World War" is sometimes attributed to Susan Rice, though we cannot confirm this. See, e.g., Mark Turn, "Africa's first world war," *Weekend Financial Times*, November 14, 1998. Also see Filip Reyntjens, *The Great African War: Congo and Regional Geopolitics, 1996-2006* (New York: Cambridge University Press, 2009), p. 198.

158 See Robert Evans, "UN Sees East Congo as Worse Crisis Than Darfur," Reuters, March 16, 2005, wherein Jan Egeland, then the head of the UN Office for the Coordination of Humanitarian Affairs, stated that "In terms of the human lives lost...this is the greatest humanitarian crisis in the world today."
< http://tinyurl.com/kyaxymc >

159 Benjamin Coghlan *et al.*, *Mortality in the Democratic Republic of Congo—An Ongoing Crisis* (International Rescue Committee and the Burnett Institute), January 22, 2008, p. ii.
< http://tinyurl.com/nt8nr5f >

160 Mahmoud Kassem *et al.*, *Final report of the Panel of Experts on the Illegal Exploitation of Natural Resources and Other Forms of Wealth of the Democratic Republic of the Congo* (S/2002/1146), October 8, 2002, para. 96. < http://tinyurl.com/lvl6xpk >

161 Coghlan *et al.*, *Mortality in the Democratic Republic of Congo*, p. ii; p. 16.

162 *Report of the Mapping Exercise documenting the most serious vio-*

lations of human rights and international humanitarian law committed within the territory of the Democratic Republic of the Congo between March 1993 and June 2003, UN High Commissioner for Human Rights, August 2010, para. 500-522; here para. 515. < http://tinyurl.com/nk6tbm3 >

163 See "Burundi Refugees and Displaced Persons: Fact Sheet," U.S. Department of State, March 14, 1994, p. 1 (as posted to the website of the National Security Archive). < http://tinyurl.com/q3n76ju >

164 United Nations High Commissioner for Refugees, *The State of the World's Refugees 1995: In search of solutions* (New York: Oxford University Press, 1995), Annexes, Table 3: "Refugee populations by country/territory of asylum and origin," and Table 4: "Largest refugee populations by country of origin," 1995. < http://www.unhcr.org/4a4c70859.html >

165 Adam Jones, *Genocide: A Comprehensive Introduction* (New York: Routledge, 1st Ed., 2006), p. 244.

166 *Ibid.*, p. 244.

167 *Ibid.*, p. 244.

168 The number of armed groups operating in Zaire-DRC these past 20 or more years is vast and confusing, and in the present account, we are going to keep the actors to an absolute minimum. But if one wants to read a catalogue of them, see Jason Stearns *et al.*, *The national army and armed groups in the eastern Congo: Untangling the Gordian knot of insecurity* (London: The Rift Valley Institute, 2013). < http://tinyurl.com/oxb5zrd >

169 Here we are drawing from Reyntjens, *The Great African War*, especially his early chapters.

170 *Ibid.*, p. 48.

171 *Ibid.*, p. 51.—For the reasons why we reject that the war in Rwanda ever was a *civil war* (i.e., non-international), see Section 2, above. On the contrary, we contend that what really happened in September 1996 was the expansion of the RPF's October 1990 invasion of Rwanda into a second-phase invasion of Zaire.

172 *Ibid.*, "U.S. Involvement," pp. 66-74.

173 Gérard Prunier, *Africa's World War: Congo, the Rwandan Genocide, and the Making of a Continental Catastrophe* (New York: Oxford

University Press, 2009), p. 127.

174 Reyntjens, *The Great African War*, p. 78.

175 John Pomfret, "Rwandans Led Revolt in Congo," *Washington Post*, July 7, 1997. < http://tinyurl.com/no6tmce >

176 Reyntjens, *The Great African War*, Ch. 3, "Massacre of Rwandan Refugees," pp. 80-101; here p. 93.

177 See Louis Charbonneau and Michelle Nichols, "Exclusive— Congo's army accused of abuse as rebels regroup in Rwanda -U.N. experts," Reuters, December 17, 2013.
< http://tinyurl.com/m2x449p >

178 Reyntjens, *The Great African War*, p. 19.

179 Philpot, *Rwanda and the New Scramble for Africa*, p. 220, based on a December 5, 2002 interview that Philpot conducted with Kengo.

180 See Mahmoud Kassem *et al.*, *Report of the Panel of Experts on the Illegal Exploitation of Natural Resources and Other Forms of Wealth of the Democratic Republic of the Congo* (S/2001/357), UN Security Council, April 12, 2001, especially para. 195-212.
< http://tinyurl.com/q6xu2zg >

181 Conservative estimates of the number of Ugandans killed under the Idi Amin dictatorship (1971-1979) are 100,000 victims, with high-end estimates at 300,000. See Richard H. Ulmann, "Human Rights and Economic Power: The United States Versus Idi Amin," *Foreign Affairs*, April, 1978. As Ulmann noted at the time, "In any contemporary lexicon of horror, Uganda is synonymous with state-become-slaughterhouse." It is all the more revealing, therefore, that given the vast body-counts we can fairly attribute to Paul Kagame's 24 year reign of terror in central Africa, first in Rwanda, and later in Zaire-DRC, his regime has never entered the contemporary lexicon of horror.

182 UN Security Council Resolution 1078 (S/RES/1078), November 9, 1996. < http://tinyurl.com/mzsg8rb >

183 UN Security Council Resolution 1080 (S/RES/1080), November 15, 1996, para. 3. < http://tinyurl.com/phkv8ys >

184 Reyntjens, *The Great African War*, pp. 86-87.

185 Philpot, *Rwanda and the New Scramble for Africa*, p. 214, based on a November 22, 2002 interview that Philpot conducted with Chré-

tien.

10. The apocryphal "Genocide Fax"

186 See n. 60, above.

187 Robin Philpot, "Rwanda, 'Shake Hands with the Devil'. General Dallaire's film fails 'Reality Check'," Global Research, November 22, 2007. < http://tinyurl.com/omonvrr >

188 Lindsey Hilsum, "UN Suppressed Warning of Rwanda Genocide Plan," *The Observer*, November 26, 1995.

189 Roméo Dallaire, "Request for Protection for Informant," UN-AMIR/Kigali, January 11, 1994 (as posted to the website of the National Security Archive) < http://tinyurl.com/kbuvlgr >

190 MRND, or *Mouvement Républicain National pour la Démocratie et le Développement*, the party of Juvénal Habyarimana. The late Joseph Nzirorera was from July 1993 on the Secretary General of the MRND. In effect, this made Nzirorera Jean-Pierre Turatsinze's boss at the MRND secretariat. According to the U.S. attorney Peter Robinson, who served as Nzirorera's lead defense counsel in the Government I trial until Nzirorea's death in July 2010, Nzirorea dismissed Turatsinze from his job with the MRND secretariat in November 1993 "because he found Turatsinze to be dishonest." Although "Turatsinze still played some role with the local Kigali MRND," more important, Robinson adds that Turatsinze was never a "top level trainer in the cadre of Interhamwe- [*sic*] armed militia of MRND." This means that the opening paragraph of the so-called "Genocide Fax" badly misidentified its "informant," and inflated his true importance. (Personal communication between Peter Robinson and David Peterson, July 22, 2014.)

191 See Dallaire, *Shake Hands with the Devil*, pp. 141-151; here pp. 142-143. In the same book, Dallaire defined the "third force" as the "Name given by UNAMIR to an extremist group that was out to derail the peace process" (p. 542). But what he really means is an extremist *Hutu* group. No consideration is given to an extremist *Tutsi* group, namely the Kagame-led RPF.

192 Gourevitch, "The Genocide Fax." < http://tinyurl.com/lxbff7t >

193 Des Forges *et al.*, *"Leave None to Tell the Story"*, pp. 150-153; here p. 151.

194 Kofi Annan, "Contacts with Informant," United Nations, New York, January 11, 1994 (as posted by to the website of the National Security Archive). < http://tinyurl.com/krdul4f >

195 See *Recommendations of the Conference Held in Kigali from November 1st to 5th, 1995, on: "Genocide, Impunity, and Accountability: Dialogue for a National and International Response,"* Office of the President, Republic of Rwanda, Kigali, December, 1995. < http://tinyurl.com/konkl9d >

196 Shaharyar M. Khan, "Warnings of Genocide to UNAMIR," MIR 3961, United Nations, November 20, 1995, para. 2.

197 N.A., "Rwanda Chronology," N.D., emphasis in the original By the presence of the handwritten name "Rivero" on the third page of this document, the "Chronology" may have been prepared by Isel Rivero, who served on the review committee, and who worked on Rwanda at the UN in New York City at the time.

198 Christopher Black, "The Dallaire Genocide Fax," Sanders Research Associates, December 7, 2005. < http://tinyurl.com/nypctau >

199 In testimony before the ICTR as recently as February 2010, Jacques-Roger Booh-Booh was asked by Prosecutor Don Webster, "Sixteen years after the genocide—you as the chief of mission of UNAMIR, a document that has generated so much controversy and so much commentary that it's used to suggest that there was a conspiracy to commit genocide—you are telling this Chamber that you didn't have the intellectual or professional curiosity to find it and read it after it's been circulating freely in the public domain for the last 10 years?" To which Booh-Booh replied: "Maybe you are in possession of that document. What I am telling you is that I only became aware of this document through rumor. What the United Nations asked me to do was to look for weapons caches in the city. I and General Dallaire went to see President Habyarimana to tell him that there are weapons that are hidden in Kigali and that the Secretary-General has asked us to tell him that he will be responsible from—for any situation arising because of those weapons

caches and that he should take action in respect of those caches and not distribute the said weapons. That is what I was asked to do and that is what I did. No one ever asked me whether Jean-Pierre had killed somebody or whether Tutsis were being killed every second or what have you." (*Prosecutor v. Édouard Karemera and Matthieu Ngirumpatse*, Case No. ICTR-98-44-T, February 17, 2010.)

200 See Jacques-Roger Booh-Booh, *"Paris n'est pas responsable du genocide,"* Le Figaro, April 11, 2005. The passage in the original reads: *"Ensuite, Hutus et Tutsis ont tout fait pour accumuler des armes dans la capitale. Le 3 mars 1994, le ministre rwandais de la Défense (hutu) m'a demandé d'autoriser son gouvernement à réceptionner du matériel de guerre en provenance d'Egypte. Je lui ai opposé un refus catégorique. Du côté des Tutsis du FPR, j'ai reçu de nombreuses informations faisant état de cargaisons d'armes qu'ils recevaient de l'Ouganda. Bizarrement, ces armes n'ont jamais été saisies par le commandant en chef de la Minuar, le général Dallaire."*

201 Amadou Deme, *Rwanda 1994 and the failure of the United Nations Mission: The whole truth* (CreateSpace Independent Publishing Platform, 2nd. Ed., 2012), p. 158.

202 Des Forges, *"Leave None To Tell the Story"*, p. 151.

203 Phil Taylor, interview with Faustin Twagiramungu, *The Taylor Report*, January 27, 2014, our transcription, picking up the program around the 35:15 mark. Later in this interview, Twagiramungu continues (from the 36:39 mark): "Let me tell you: If it was a case of planning to kill Tutsis, why did not…General Dallaire, why did not he inform the people who were in CND, I mean the RPF soldiers who were there? Why? He should have informed them….Why one has to keep this planning for genocide [secret] from January to April? Why? Why? Why UN did it? If you know that this planning was there, and kept this information until the genocide took place? No no. There is something wrong, I think. Fortunately, we are still alive to tell the truth." < http://tinyurl.com/ouwnm96 >

204 Deme, *Rwanda 1994 and the failure of the United Nations Mission*, p. 56.

205 Judge Erik Møse *et al., Judgment, Prosecutor v. Théoneste Bagosora*

et al., Case No. ICTR-98-41-T, December 18, 2008, para. 2103. < http://tinyurl.com/ncarqtd >.

11. The *New York Times* and other "Genocide Fax" disinformants

206 See n. 3, above.
207 See Rafael Medoff, "The Rwandan Genocide," *New York Times*, January 11, 2014, < http://tinyurl.com/kyg4qvx >; Karel Kovanda, "Tracing the Rwanda 'Genocide Fax'," *New York Times*, January 15, 2014, < http://tinyurl.com/mcqxrte >; and Linda Melvern, Gregory Stanton, and nine others, "The Rwandan Genocide," *New York Times*, January 22, 2014. < http://tinyurl.com/lne5lpl >
208 Melvern and Stanton *et al.* < http://tinyurl.com/lne5lpl >
209 See *Rwanda: The Preventable Genocide*, Ch. 9, "The Eve of the Genocide: What the World Knew," pp. 54-63, here p. 59. It is interesting that two of the sources this report cites when discussing the "Genocide Fax" are Human Rights Watch's Alison Des Forges and Philip Gourevitch. < http://tinyurl.com/lvrotjb >
210 Dobbs, "Rwanda's Shrouded Nightmare."
< http://tinyurl.com/k2ze336 >
211 Gerald Caplan, "Inflammatory falsehood poor homage to twentieth anniversary of Rwanda genocide," *Rabble.ca*, February 24, 2014. < http://tinyurl.com/mdh2mp7 >. For Michael Dobbs's treatment of the "Genocide Fax" at the Holocaust Memorial Museum's website, see "Genocide Fax." < http://tinyurl.com/pgdgnrk >
212 See Section 7 as well as "Appendix I: More on the 'conspiracy to commit genocide' that never was."
213 See Edward S. Herman and David Peterson, "George Monbiot and the *Guardian* on 'Genocide Denial' and "Revisionism'," *MRZine*, September 2, 2011. < http://tinyurl.com/3t7tq4h >
214 See Reyntjens, *Political Governance in Post-Genocide Rwanda*, Ch. 5, "Dealing with the World and the Region," pp. 124-162.

12. Role of UN, human rights groups, media, and intellectuals in

promulating the standard model

215 See n. 146, above.

216 UN Security Council Resolution 2150 (S/RES/2150), April 16, 2014, para. 1. < http://tinyurl.com/lty6s3a >

217 *Threats to international peace and security: Prevention and fight against genocide* (S/PV.7155), UN Security Council, April 16, 2014. < http://tinyurl.com/mo6mkco >

218 Resolution 2150, quoting the introductory paragraphs and para. 2.

219 "UN Security Council and US Senate Pass Resolutions on the Prevention of Genocide," United States Holocaust Historical Museum website, April 21, 2014. < http://tinyurl.com/lcvgzlb >

220 This pattern is uniform.—When as recently as late August 2013, the United States began threatening Syria with a possible military attack after the still-unsolved August 22 sarin gas incidents in the suburbs east of Damascus, Human Rights Watch and Amnesty International issued the following statements. "Human Rights Watch does not take a position advocating or opposing such intervention, but any armed intervention should be judged by how well it protects all Syrian civilians from further atrocities…. If there is a military intervention, all warring parties must strictly adhere to the laws of war." ("Statement on Possible Intervention in Syria," Human Rights Watch, August 28, 2014. < http://tinyurl.com/oxllbbg >) "Amnesty International generally neither condemns nor condones the resort to the use of force in international relations, nor does it make any comments or pass judgment on the arguments justifying the use of force… In the event of armed international intervention, Amnesty International's focus will be on the conduct of such intervention in the light of the rules of international humanitarian law and applicable human rights law. ("Questions and Answers," Amnesty International, August 29, 2013, p. 3. < http://tinyurl.com/pl3tn3w >)

221 See n. 60, above.

222 B.W. Ndiaye *et al., Question of the Violation of Human Rights and Fundamental Freedoms in Any Part of the World, with Particular Reference to Colonial and Other Dependent Countries and Territories* (E/CN.4/1994/7/Add.1), Economic and Social Council, August

11, 1993, Section 11, "The genocide question," para. 78-81. < http://tinyurl.com/pr2ksxs >

223 Des Forges, *"Leave None To Tell the Story"*, p. 53.

224 Factiva database searches under the "Wires," "Newspapers: All," and "Transcripts" categories carried out on May 23, 2014 for the period October 1, 1990 through April 30, 2014. Our search parameters were: *rst=(twir or tnwp or ttpt) and rwanda* and alison des forges*.

225 See Philpot, *Rwanda and the New Scramble for Africa*, Appendix II, pp. 265-269. Therein, Jérôme C. Bicamumpaka, the Rwandan interim government's minister of foreign affairs from April 9 until mid-July 1994, recounts how in May 1994, when his delegation traveled to the United Nations in New York City to lobby it to help curb the violence then engulfing his country, Alison Des Forges mobilized a counter-offensive to prevent the UN and the relevant ambassadors from meeting with him.

226 *Ibid.*, p. 87, and n. 13, p. 243. This information is drawn from Des Forges's *Curriculum Vitae, ca.* late 1994, which she submitted to Canada's Minister of Citizenship and Immigration when she served as an "expert witness" before this body in its 1995 deportation hearings of the Hutu exile Léon Mugesera, who had fled Rwanda for Canada in late 1992. Of course, Des Forges testified *against* Mugesera.

227 Des Forges, *"Leave None To Tell the Story"*, pp. 65-95.

228 *Ibid.*, pp. 65-66. On the presence of clandestine RPF cells in Kigali and elsewhere, see n. 50, above.

229 *Ibid.*, p. 66.

230 *Ibid.*, p. 76.

231 See n. 7, above.

232 Gourevitch, *We wish to inform you that...*, p. 356, were the name "Elizabeth Rubin" appears.

233 Gourevitch quotes with disapproval a line from Filip Reyntjens, who had told an interviewer: "It's not a story of good guys and bad guys. It's a story of bad guys. Period." (*Ibid.*, pp. 185-186.)

234 *Ibid.*, p. 274.

235 *Ibid.*, Ch. 13, pp. 185-208

236 *Ibid.*, p. 203.

237 See Pottier, *Re-imagining Rwanda*, pp. 156-170; especially pp. 166-170. Pottier specifically criticizes Gourevitch's misrepresentations of the Kibeho massacre: "His story is a *chef d'oeuvre* of obfuscation" (p. 169).

238 Gourevitch, *We wish to inform you that…*, pp. 266-273.

239 Paul Kagame's perspective was greatly enhanced by a long, uncritical interview that the journal *Foreign Affairs* published in 2014. See "Rebooting Rwanda: A Conversation With Paul Kagame," *Foreign Affairs*, May/June, 2014.
< http://tinyurl.com/nwtvhl9 >

240 Factiva database byline-searches of a selective list of 40 potential contributors to any debate on the "Rwandan genocide," carried out on May 22, 2014 for the period April 1, 2004 through April 30, 2014. Our search parameters were: *by=[soandso] and Rwanda* and genocide**. The way we designed our byline-searches, it would have been sufficient for any of the 40 potential contributors to have published something either in print or online in which the words "Rwanda" or "Rwandan" and "genocide" or "genocidal" appear in the same item. We then checked each item to determine that the contributor had asserted something about the "Rwandan genocide;" if the contributor did not, we excluded the item from the reported total. We should also add that some of the reported total includes items in which the "Rwandan genocide" was mentioned merely in passing, without being the focus of the contributor; these items were included in the reported total.

241 See Paul Kagame, "Reflecting on Rwanda's Past—While Looking Ahead," *Wall Street Journal*, April 7, 2014.
< http://tinyurl.com/qcg3l9b >

242 During our ten-year search period, Pierre Péan's byline on the "Rwandan genocide" has appeared nine times in the French media: *Libération* (2), *Le Point* (1), *Marianne* (1), *Le Nouveau Marianne* (3), and *Marianne2* (2).

Concluding Note: Genocidist misallocation (Rwanda) and the real

genocide denial (DRC)

243 Power, *"A Problem from Hell"*, p. 503.

244 To be precise, 104 days: April 6 through July 18, 1994.

245 Ban Ki-moon, "Remarks at the commemoration of the 20th anniversary of the Rwandan genocide," UN Secretary-General, April 7, 2014. < http://tinyurl.com/lzjus59 >

246 Kiran Moodley, "Bill Clinton: we could have saved 300,000 lives in Rwanda," CNBC Meets, March 13, 2013.
< http://www.cnbc.com/id/100546207 >

247 See the entry for "Democratic Republic of Congo" at the website of the International Criminal Court. At this time of writing, the six DRC-related indictees have been: Thomas Lubanga Dyilo (convicted), Germain Katanga (convicted), Mathieu Ngudjolo Chui (acquitted), Bosco Ntaganda (no trial yet), Callixte Mbarushimana (court declined to confirm the charges against him), and Sylvestre Mudacumura (still at large). < http://tinyurl.com/o92shku >

248 See Herman and Peterson, *The Politics of Genocide, passim.*—We should add that in a major study of the International Criminal Court published in 2014, David Hoile makes a point that we ourselves have made before, namely, that "The ICC has charged thirty-two people to date. They are all Africans." (*Justice Denied: The Reality of the International Criminal Court* (London: The Africa Research Center, 2014), pp. 199-227; here p. 203.) But even more revealing about the reality of the ICC than its "exclusive focus on Africa," has been which kind of African leaders the ICC has not focused on. The fact that the ICC could indict Sudan's Omar al-Bashir, the Côte d'Ivoire's Laurent Gbagbo, Kenya's Uhuru Kenyatta, and Libya's Muammar Gaddafi, but not Rwanda's Paul Kagame, and not Uganda's Yoweri Museveni, shows us that the ICC's focus is not just on Africans, but on those Africans who are not allies/clients of the United States.

249 Quoted in "Ought King Leopold To Be Hanged?" a 1905 interview with the Reverend John N. Harris by the British journalist W.T. Stead, published as a Supplement to Mark Twain's sarcastic, anti-colonial pamphlet, *King Leopold's Soliloquy: A Defense of His Congo Rule* (Boston: P.R. Warren Co., 2nd Ed., 1905), p. 56.

< http://tinyurl.com/nr97o6z >

250 What we here refer to as a *"victims'" license to go right on killing* is often referred to as a "genocide credit," but we prefer our formulation.

251 Paul Kagame, "Speech by President Paul Kagame at the 20th Commemoration of the Genocide Against the Tutsi," Kwibuka20, April 7, 2014. < http://www.kwibuka.rw/speech >

Appendix I: More on the alleged Hutu "conspiracy to commit genocide" that never was

252 *The Prosecutor v. Edouard Karemera et al.*, Oral Summary, Case No. ICTR-98-44-T, International Criminal Tribunal for Rwanda, December 21, 2011, para. 75. < http://tinyurl.com/m7ox2od > For the remainder of Government I, see Judge Dennis C.M. Byron *et al., Judgment, Prosecutor v. André Rwamakuba*, Case No. ICTR-98-44C-I, September 20, 2006, p. 86. < http://tinyurl.com/k5o94c2 >. In this Judgment, the Trial Chamber acknowledged that it had been the Prosecution itself, as early as 2004, that removed the initial "conspiracy to commit genocide" charge from its Indictment against Rwamakuba (para. 21-22).

253 CDR, or *Coalition pour la Défense de la République*, a Hutu political party to the right of Habyarimana's MRND.

254 Judge Fausto Pocar *et al., Judgment on Appeal, Ferdinand Nahimana et al. v. The Prosecutor*, Case No. ICTR-99-52-A, November 28, 2007, para. 912, p. 292. < http://tinyurl.com/ljm5lyj >

255 See n. 146, above.

256 Judge William H. Sekule, *Judgment, Prosecutor v. Pauline Nyiramasuhuko et al.*, Case No. ICTR-98-42-T, June 24, 2011, para. 6186, pp. 1449-1451.—At this time of writing, all six defendants' cases were on appeal at the ICTR. < http://tinyurl.com/n6k63xz >

257 Møse *et al., Judgment, Prosecutor v. Théoneste Bagosora et al.*, para. 2084-2113, pp. 531-540; here para. 2109, 2110, and 2112, pp. 539-540. < http://tinyurl.com/ncarqtd >

258 See Peter Erlinder *et al., Major Aloys Ntabakuze Amended Final*

Trial Brief, May 27, 2007, as archived at the website of the Rwanda Documents Project. < http://tinyurl.com/moam95e > In particular, see Part Three, Section II, "Alternative Explanation of the Tragic Events in Rwanda During the Four Year War," pp. 138-174.

< http://tinyurl.com/ow3tedn > This argument is reprised at greater length in Erlinder, The *Accidental... Genocide, passim.*

< http://tinyurl.com/k2opuat > Separately, Erlinder has written: "The only way the ICTR 'victors' court' could be forced to 'give-up' endorsement of the 'Hutu conspiracy to commit genocide' charge was by presenting the presiding Judge Møse with an alternative explanation that was just as plausible, or more so, so that 'a reasonable fact-finder could not hold beyond a reasonable doubt that there was only one alternative....'. Because that is a universal legal principle the Judges could not openly get around. *That* was the strategy. A credible 'non-conspiracy' explanation prevented conspiracy convictions as a matter of law, even though 'genocide' had been judicially noticed." (Personal Communication between Peter Erlinder and David Peterson, July 12, 2014.)

259 See Dallaire, *Shake Hands with the Devil*, pp. 357-358. Although the date is unclear, Dallaire recounts a meeting with Kagame "in newly held territory" in the Byumba prefecture, where "Kagame had set up a tactical headquarters that was much easier to reach than his compound in Mulindi." "I raised with the general my worries about the fate of the Tutsis and the moderate Hutus still marooned in the Mille Collines," Dallaire writes. Kagame replied: "There will be many sacrifices in this war. If the refugees have to be killed for the cause, they will be considered as having been part of the sacrifice" (p. 358).

Appendix II: The apocryphal "Genocide Fax"—another look

260 Gourevitch, "The Genocide Fax." < http://tinyurl.com/lxbff7t >
261 See n. 190 above. According to an affidavit filed by Jean-Pierre Turatsinze's widow, Genevieve, with investigators for the International Criminal Tribunal for Rwanda, in early 1994, Jean-Pierre traveled to Tanzania, where members of his family were then living, "some

of [whom] were RPF members. They are the ones who convinced [Jean-Pierre] to join the RPF." (Affidavit of Genevieve Turatsinze, International Criminal Tribunal for Rwanda, April 3, 2003. < http://tinyurl.com/kbsoasp >) However, as noted above, we suspect that Jean-Pierre had already been working covertly on behalf of the RPF by the date of his first contact with UNAMIR staff, *ca.* January 10, 1994.

262 Dobbs, "The Rwanda 'Genocide Fax': What We Know Now." < http://tinyurl.com/l7p3yl6 >.

263 Note well that in the version of the "Genocide Fax" that we reproduce here and refer to as Copy C or as the Connaughton Fax, the date-stamp has been enhanced by a professional graphic designer for the sake of its legibility, but its original font (Bauhaus Medium) as well as its actual content (discussed in this Appendix as well as Section 10) remain exactly as they appeared across the top of the original fax to the DPKO, dated November 27, 1995.

264 Khan, "Warnings of Genocide to UNAMIR," para. 2.

265 Ralph Zacklin, *Re: Prosecutor v. Augustin Ndindiliyimana* (ICTR-00-56-T), Office of Legal Counsel, United Nations, New York, August 11, 2004, p. 1, emphasis added. Also see Black, "The Dallaire Genocide Fax." < http://tinyurl.com/nypctau >

266 Gourevitch, "The Genocide Fax," p. 42. < http://tinyurl.com/lxbff7t >

INDEX

Kayonga, Charles, 99*n*70
Kengo, Leon, 53
Kesteloot, Henry, 62
Khan, Shaharyar, 58, 59, 87, 88–89
Kibeho refugee camp, 70, 121*n*237
Kigali, safe sport for RPF in, 21,
    22–23, 29
Ki-moon, Ban, 74
Kingdom of Rwanda, 14–15, 16
Kinyarwanda (language), 14
Kinzer, Stephen, 93*n*30
Kouchner, Bernard, 100–101*n*85

Laughland, John, 41, 106*n*124
"*Leave None to Tell the Story*" (Des
    Forges and Human Rights Watch),
    57–58, 68
Lemarchand, René, 20
Lenin, V. I., 69
Leopold II (king of Belgium), 76, 77
Libération (French newspaper), 47
Lizinde, Théoneste, 28, 29
Logiest, Guy, 16
Lyons, James, 29, 99*n*69

Mamdani, Mahmood, 15
maps
    Africa, 9
    DRC, 49
    Rwanda, 10, 49
Marchal, Luc, 62
Mbarushimana, Callixte, 122*n*247
MDR (*Mouvement Démocratique
    Républicain*), 62, 109–110*n*145
media
    advocates vs. dissenters of stan-
        dard model in, 70–73, 72*t*
    bias of, 12–13, 70–73
    "conspiracy" lie disseminated
        by, 46
    Des Forges's influence in, 67–69
    earliest use of "Rwandan geno-
        cide" by, 97*n*61
    ICTR trial related to, 80–81

Kagame-Power flattery in,
    100–101*n*85
number of articles on Rwanda,
    71, 72*t*, 121*n*240
threats against Mobutu in, 51–52
See also disinformants; propa-
    ganda system; *and specific
    newspapers*
Melvern, Linda
    as "Genocide Fax" disinformant,
        63–64
    on Hutu extremists, 31
    on Kambanda's ICTR trial, 40, 41
    media access of, 71, 73
    standard model promoted by, 6,
        71
Military I and II trials
    conspiracy model demolished
        in, 46
    defendants listed, 109*n*143
    "Genocide Fax" presented and
        dismissed at, 59–60, 63
    Hourigan's memo in evidentiary
        record, 98–99*n*68
    Ndindiliyimana's attorney at, 59,
        86, 88, 107*n*133
    summary of judgments, 78–79
Milken Institute Global Conference
    (Los Angeles), 13
Mobutu Sese Seko, 51–52, 53, 54,
    112*n*156
De Morgen (Belgian newspaper), 56
Møse (judge), 124*n*258
*Mouvement Démocratique Républi-
    cain* (MDR), 62, 109–110*n*145
MRND (*Mouvement Républicain
    National pour la Démocratie et le
    Développement*), 57, 62, 78, 88,
    109–110*n*145, 115*n*190. *See also*
    Interahamwe
Mucchielli, Roger, 69
Mucyo, Jean de Dieu, 102*n*92
Mudacumura, Sylvestre, 122*n*247
Mugenzi, Justin, 80, 109*n*143

134

publicity about Hutu refugees'
plight and, 54–55
RPF's aggression ignored by, 22
Rwandan seat on, 39
specific resolutions
827, 96n54
955, 26–27, 38, 39, 75
1078, 54
1080, 54–55
2150, 66–67
standard model promoted by, 7,
66–67
United States
anti-Mobutu policy of, 52–53
Arusha Accords and, 19
attacks on other countries by, 67,
119n220
"conspiracy" lie disseminated
by, 45
Des Forges's connections to security agencies of, 68
geopolitical power of, 12–13
ICTR prosecutor removed at behest of, 42–43
Kagame-RPF support from, 18–
19, 31–32, 35, 36–38, 48–49,
52–55, 74–75
political support for "civil war,"
24–25
RPF's aggression ignored by,
22–23
UN influenced by, 66–67
war crimes ambassador of, 42, 43
See also West
U.S. Army Command and Staff College (Fort Leavenworth), 18
U.S. Holocaust Memorial Museum,
11–12, 64–65, 67, 86
U.S. State Department, 37
University of Michigan, GenoDynamics research project, 32–34
UPDF (Ugandan People's Defense
Force, formerly Ugandan National
Resistance Army), 14, 18, 23–24,

61, 93–94n31. *See also* Rwandan
Patriotic Front

"victims'" license (genocide credit),
76, 123n250
victor's justice, 38–43, 124n258

Wall Street Journal, 72
war. *See* armed conflicts; *and specific forces*
Washington Post, 53, 68
Watson, Catharine, 17, 94n33
Webster, Don, 116–117n199
West (U.S. and allies)
African leaders protected by,
122n248
alleged failure to protect Rwandan people, 11, 12, 35–38
"conspiracy" lie disseminated by,
44–46, 63–73
DRC resources eyed by, 53
ethnocentrism of, 111n147
evidence of Kagame-RPF's responsibility for assassinations
buried by, 27–28, 30–32
Kagame and RPF support from,
18–19, 31–32, 35, 36–38,
48–49, 52–55, 74–75
political support for "civil war,"
24–25
prosecution for killings in DRC
and interests of, 75–76
responsible for genocide, 22–23,
44, 46
revisionism-before-the-fact tactic
of, 25–26
Tutsi exiles to, 17
UN influenced by, 66–67
Yugoslavia's dissolution fostered
by, 25–26
See also Arusha Accords; "conspiracy to exterminate Tutsi";
propaganda system; standard
model of Rwandan genocide;